MICHAEL PRAGER

FAT BOY
THIN MAN

ISBN 978-0-9826720-0-6

Book and jacket design: Meg Dreyer | artifactsartifictions.com

For G. and J.

CONTENTS

ACKNOWLEDGEMENTS

I WOULDN'T HAVE THIS STORY had I not become an addict, come to understand the implications of being an addict, and been helped to see all the ways in which I was hurting myself. These discoveries were sometimes led by professionals, but most of the insight came from fellow searchers and sufferers whom I met in rehab, therapy groups, and support groups. We helped each other greatly, and I'm grateful for all the sharing; this book is one product of it.

Writing the book was not my idea. Oddly, it existed as a complete thought in the minds of two valued counselors years before I started typing. In fact, when each of them suggested it to me, separately but in the same neighborhood of time, I had no interest whatsoever. I wasn't sure I'd even want to read such a book, never mind write it.

I wouldn't say I ever followed their suggestion, either, although the facts that they don't know each other, and that they broached the idea in the same general way — not, "Why don't you write a book?" or "If you were going to write a book, what might it say?" but "When are you going to write your book?" as if it already existed — did gnaw at me as time passed.

The two counselors are Kris White of Mystical Therapies of Haverhill, Mass., and Linda Boynton, a therapist in private practice in Boston. (Contact information for both is in Appendix B.) I have been relying on Linda's bedrock insights and mountaineer charms for more than a decade. She is strongly empathic, encyclopedic in memory, and extremely compassionate. When she tells me things about me, I give them credence, even if I don't recognize what she's saying as true. They often turn out to be.

Although our conversations tend more toward spiritual than practical, I trust Kris, too. I find comfort from talking with her, and she too turns out to be correct when I'm sure she can't be.

What got me to the keyboard was the birth of the Food Addiction Institute of Sarasota, Fla. I was invited to attend an organizing session by Phil Werdell of Acorn Food Dependency Recovery Services, who has gone from eating-issues counselor to good friend and writing colleague. Three of us at the meeting — the other was Colleen Hillock of Medicine Hat, Alberta, Canada — argued that public education should be a top priority of the institute, so, of course, we were assigned to the task. After we caucused, one of my assignments was to write about 15 pages on my story of overcoming extreme obesity; when I'd reached 25 pages and felt I had only begun, I realized I had plenty to say. Though we accomplished several things, we haven't yet carried the institute's message to the public; over time, we have come to think that this book might achieve that.

Phil offered patronage during the time we worked together, but he has also offered unstinting encouragement and guidance. Outside my family, Phil has done more to support me than just about anyone, in every way. Additionally, though all the ideas in this book speak for me, many were broached, influenced, and/or broadened by Phil; he has been both guide and sounding board.

Theresa Wright and I have a similar story. I went to her for a food plan, and she continues to advise me. But we've become friendly over time and we try to speak every couple of weeks. We have also collaborated professionally, and she contributed feedback on early drafts and the best suggestion I received for this version.

Other food-addiction professionals have lent guidance and support, including Marty Lerner, Joan Ifland, Brenda Iliff, and Lori Herold. Joe Frascella, a director at the National Institute on Drug Abuse, has been both gracious and encouraging. Jeffrey Grimm of Western Washington U. and Richard Johnson of the University of Colorado in Denver are top-flight researchers who've found time to offer support and guidance.

I have consulted with many journalists and other writers during the book's creation. I'm grateful to Mike Waller, Dan Haar, Ann Marsh, Deb Hagen, Deborah Jacobs, Jean Fain, Alison Bass, Geoff Edgers, Alyssa Haywoode and Linda Wertheimer, Jeffrey Marx, Peter Zheutlin, Sam Nejame, Steve Maas, and Alison Lobron and Cam Terwilliger, my teachers at Grub Street, the nonprofit arts group in Boston. My fellow students were constructive and inspiring.

I'm also grateful to writer Kay Sheppard and agent Geri Thoma, which must be unusual if not a first: thanking an agent who declined to represent me. Even so, her reactions were helpful and useful.

I thank my parents for their forbearance; there is plenty in this book they think is nobody else's business, and would strongly have preferred that I not have mentioned them.

Meg Dreyer designed both the book and the web site, which was programmed by Eddie Monroe. Both brought great spirit, energy, and skill to the project, and I appreciate their aid and expertise.

I have had a number of readers, probably too many for my own good, but that reflects on me, not them. My friend and former colleague David Mehegan gave a thoughtful and authoritative early review, and I have returned to Margaret Ann Brady repeatedly and reliably. Other helpful readers have included my wife, Georgina Fulton Prager; my brother Richard Prager and his family: Beverly, Sarah, and Alex; my father-in-law Claiborne Wilkinson; and close friends Ron Turmaine and Shelley Fried. My brother-in-law, Doug Fulton, has been a bulwark of bonhomie and support.

In addition to her editorial guidance, Georgie is in many ways responsible for my completing the book. She made my mission ours, has provided intellectual and emotional ballast when I was foundering, and has not wavered in her belief in me. I love her and do not know where I would be without her.

MICHAEL PRAGER
JUNE 2010

FOREWORD

HERE IS OUR CHANCE TO MEET and to know Michael as he progresses in the disease of food addiction, surrenders to that fact, and learns to enjoy the progression of recovery. Within these pages he shares his experience, strength, and hope with us as he faces the baffling illness we call food addiction.

From childhood until he entered treatment at 365 pounds, Michael was trapped by a relentless compulsion to eat huge amounts of addictive trigger foods. His story tells us certain foods can be as addictive as cocaine, nicotine, or alcohol. Addicted to multiple substances, he was surrounded by family and friends who were also trapped in addiction. During the course of his addiction he discovered that mainstream medicine offers no effective or safe treatment for the obese and suffering food addict.

Michael allows us to see his soul — the soul of a tormented addict. Isolated and ostracized, he shares the pain of never fitting in or feeling part of his community. His life became a roller coaster ride. "Bright and sunshiny" or "dark enough to suck the sunshine from the room," as he described himself, his colleagues never knew which Michael they were going to get.

Then one day in October 1991 his world changed. At first resistant and reluctant, he learned to walk a different path. On that path he met the people who were to show him how to recover from the relentless disease of mind and body that had ruled his life. He tells us that his path is now a spiritual one. From doubter to a man of faith and prayer, he asks God's help to be "patient, tolerant, loving, and kind."

Beautifully written, often painfully honest, this is the most important work of this journalist's life. It has been a privilege to meet you, Michael! Thanks for sharing your life with us.

KAY SHEPPARD

Kay Sheppard, MA, is a licensed mental health counselor and a certified eating disorder specialist. Since the early 1980s she has pioneered in the development of the concept of food addiction and has helped thousands recover, based on the theory that for some people, refined and processed foods can be as addictive as alcohol and other drugs. Her best-selling books "Food Addiction: The Body Knows," "From the First Bite," "A Complete Guide to Recovery from Food Addiction," and "Food Addiction: Healing Day by Day," have become primary resources for food addicts, their families and addiction professionals. Sheppard is an internationally recognized consultant, trainer, and therapist who conducts workshops for food addicts and professionals worldwide. She has an online support recovery forum with a membership of more than 5,000 men and women at www.kaysheppard.com.

PROLOGUE

A 365-POUND GUY WALKS INTO A SUB SHOP, with or without mustard stains on his sweater, and orders a couple of foot-longs. Anyone in the place is going to think they're all for him, no matter what he does. That's why, sometimes, I'd just go in and order, and let 'em think what they wanted. But sometimes I'd go with the list. I'd grab a scrap of paper off the floor of my car and scribble on it, or write it out as if it were real, in case the clerk grabbed it to check for grammar or something. Then I'd roll out the driver's side door and roll on inside.

"Foot-long roast beef with onions and mayo, please."

I always got that one, that one was "mine." I've never understood why, for me, onions harmonize so perfectly with the richness of mayo when melded with rare, thinly sliced beef, but it had been scratching an itch since junior high. But the others were optional. If I went for the meatballs, I'd add only cheese — extra cheese — and I didn't care if I had to pay extra for it. If it was the tuna, I'd go for everything except olives. If it was the Italian cold cuts, I might even get the olives — everyone knew I didn't like olives, so that would help prove that it wasn't for me. I might even add that to the repartee: "I hate olives, man, but he wants them."

"He" didn't exist, of course, but I needed him nevertheless, to explain why I was ordering so much food. The key to the repartee was to be offhand. Casual comments, and not too many, so it was conversational without being obvious. If I went on too long, there was always the hazard of being caught in the lie, too, though as long as I got in and got out, I usually got by.

There was a temptation to stay sometimes, especially if I got a talkative guy like Scott, who owned the Subway on Farmington Avenue in Hartford. He was a young guy — younger than me, anyway — and seemed bent on building an empire based on carefully controlled portions and freshly baked bread. I wouldn't be surprised if he made it, either. I remember how he'd take the time to carefully rotate each tube of dough in its perforated slot in the baking tray, after proofing but before baking. He was a smart guy, too: certainly smart enough to know what I was doing, and smart enough not to let on, even with a smirk.

Especially with a smirk. I'd more likely have rejected a place for that than I would have for questionable cleanliness or the orange-yellow patina that mayo develops when it hasn't been properly chilled. We never got to be friends, certainly, but we'd get into conversation sometimes: the Sox, or the weather, or the milder reaches of politics. For me, it might be the only companionship I'd get outside of work for days. The problem was that I couldn't start eating while we talked, and once I had my stuff, I really didn't want to wait.

If the ruse was going to work, of course, I was compelled to get a bag of chips for each sandwich. Just as I varied the condiments, I'd vary the varieties — usually a bag of plain, and then some salt-and-vinegar or Cheetos or whatever. I liked most of them, and besides, I never combo-ed sandwiches and chips the way I married onions and mayo. By rights, I should have also bought a soda for every sandwich — what were my pals, or colleagues, or family, or whomever supposed to drink with their meals? But there were limits to my lying: dropping ten bucks on a snack was one thing, but the sodas would be another three, and I didn't want them besides. They would only take up room I wanted for food, and if they were fountain drinks, I couldn't even save them for later.

I'd usually dig into the bag as soon as I was out of sight of the shop, for chips if not for a sandwich. The choice would depend on several factors, such as how long it had been since I'd eaten, and how far I had to go before I arrived. One of the reasons for buying multiples, whether it was sandwiches or loaves of cinnamon-raisin bread at the day-old store, was to have something for the ride home without running out once I'd got there.

For a good 20 years, that's as much thinking as I put into my habit — staying stocked up while staying below the radar. But by the late 1980s, during a very slow awakening to reality prompted by therapy, the love of family, and the decency of others, I began to understand what I was doing to myself, and that if I didn't make changes, nothing was going to change. That's not to say I actually changed, however. I observed, interpreted, and commented — as if they were actions. For better than a year afterward, I continued on the same path, though at least with increasing awareness of what was going on. I particularly remember driving down Gillett Street in the dark one night, cutting through from Farmington to Asylum Avenue on my way home from Subway. All of the sudden I recognized what I was feeling, and I broke out in guffaws. I had just visited my dealer, I had my drug, and I was set for the night. And my amusement went one better: unlike when I'd scored pot or cocaine, I didn't even have to worry about the cops.

1

So What Are We Talking About, Anyway?

MOST PEOPLE WHO PICK UP BOOKS about dramatic weight loss want a fix, for themselves or for a loved one. They want to be told what to do. They want a guru.

Well, I'm no guru. I created practically none of the measures that have transformed me from a hapless, isolated 365-pounder to a happy, normal-bodied family man. I have benefited from the loving guidance of others. Even so, my experiences have left me with bits of wisdom, and that's why I've written this book — to share attitudes, ideas, and behaviors that were shared with me, and that have worked.

Those are two key concepts: First, that they worked. For so much of my life, being "right" was my prime value, having failed to understand that being right and fat, right and lonely, right and miserable, was hollow achievement. Now, I see that the only useful standard is, am I better off?

For comparison, consider what cancer patients do: If so advised, they accept injections of poison or bombardments of radiation, putting up with nausea, fatigue, hair loss. They're high prices, but judged to be worth paying, even for the hope of overcoming the problem. And second, that I'm sharing them, not top-down but as they were shared with me, by people who had more experience, knowledge, and success than I'd had. Claiming gurudom would clearly flout that spirit.

Not only that, but I might not know what is best for you! That's why I don't — and won't — prescribe.

But I do feel qualified to relate my experience, and feel confident it will help others who attempt a similar path. Why am I so confident? Simply because I'm not so special, so anything that worked for me will probably work for others.

That's one of my bits of wisdom, and is quite unlike the attitude I had in the days leading to Oct. 21, 1991, when I entered the eating disorders unit of South Oaks, a psychiatric hospital on Long Island. I was a 34-year old fat man who'd been a fat kid, a fat teen, and a fat 20-something.

My favorite foods had changed over time, but my desire for volume had been constant for at least 15 years. I'd begun dieting at 10 or 11, and had been shipped away to fat-boy camp for three of my teen-age summers, to no lasting avail. I was a serial 100-pound loser who'd always gained back more. I'd been sneered at, taunted, pitied, and patronized.

My personal life had been middling at best, filled with troubled family relationships and friends who'd favored the same illegal drugs I did. At work, I'd had some success but kept getting busted in rank because I couldn't get along with people, which was as much a sign of my stumbling as my copious fat; if only weight had been my only problem!

I'd thought that I could handle my needs, that I just had to be a little more clever and all would be well, even though my cleverness had wrought little. Incredibly, I'd also thought that I knew what was best for others, and wasn't reluctant to share my wisdom, invited or not.

People don't like that, it turns out.

Just because I try not to tell individuals what to do, though, doesn't mean I don't have opinions about what being obese is like, what non-obese people don't understand about obesity, and the roles that all Americans contribute to the obesity epidemic, which public-health officials call the second-most cause of preventable death. Here are some of them:

MAINSTREAM AMERICA, INCLUDING MEDICINE, HAS NO SOLUTION FOR OBESITY, OR EVEN OVERWEIGHT. Yeah, that has the flaws of most sweeping statements, but look at the numbers: Since 1960, obesity among American adults has gone from 13 percent to over 30 percent, and overweight has gone from less than half to about two-thirds. And yet, in that time, attitudes haven't budged. The mainstream still considers obesity to be a moral failing, and still thinks that The Zone, or Atkins, or Weight Watchers, or Jenny Direct, or fat-burning pills, jaw wiring or stomach stapling is an answer. These "solutions" have been around for decades, and yet the problem not only isn't receding, it's exploding. It's as though we're under mass hypnosis, unable to perceive what we see on every street, in every mall, at every restaurant.

PEOPLE WHO SAY DIETS DON'T WORK ARE MISSING THE POINT. I've lost more than 500 pounds on diets, so they do "work," if your only goal is to lose weight — and for most people who've ever dieted, that was the only goal. The defect in that approach, of course, is that "diets," as we define them, are a temporary measure.

If the weight gain owes to a temporary condition — overeating as the result of grief, or overused out of boredom during a convalescence, or the short-term use of a drug that has weight gain as a side effect — then a short-term change might be an appropriate resolution.

But if overweight or obesity has longer-lasting or systemic causes, of which there are many, then it is foolish to expect that a temporary change will do any more than give temporary relief. That's just obvious, isn't it?

MOST OBESE PEOPLE NEED MORE THAN WEIGHT LOSS TO BE HEALTHY. The first time I lost more than 100 pounds, I was in high school, and I thought that once I'd lost the weight, my troubles would be over: Girls would accept me. Guys would count me as one of them. My sense of isolation would fade, and my talents would become obvious.

But no; I just lost weight and learned that weight wasn't the problem. If anything, removing the barrier that fat had served physically exposed me more than I'd ever been, and when people stopped telling me how great I was for losing my weight, I started gaining it back.

I needed all sorts of help, which I eventually found in individual and group therapy, in more intensive counseling venues, and in peer-support groups. But back then, I didn't have a clue.

I'm convinced that for many overweight people, and for the strong majority of obese people, weight is a symptom of other problems. Clearly, overweight is a threat to health all by itself, but if its causes extend to more than eating, then its solution will have to include more than dieting.

Again, this is just plainer than plain, is it not?

ADDICTION IS A HUGE FACTOR IN OBESITY. I have advocated for the concept of food addiction in newspapers and magazines, and am repeatedly impressed by how the notion horrifies chatroom commenters. Some of the reaction arises from political outlook, some from prejudice, and some from other forms of ignorance. It's OK; I'm here to help:

➤ Not all fat people are food addicts. Not even most of them. But extrapolating statistics from alcoholism and drug addiction, we can conservatively estimate that more than 12 million American adults are food addicts. My opinion is that there are many more.

I believe that the methods that have helped me enjoy almost 20 years of serenity and happiness in a normal-sized body, after three decades of freakish, debilitating obesity, would work for the vast majority of people who struggle with weight. But for the least affected, this kit of solutions would amount to what the writer Theodore Bernstein termed "atomic fly swatters," effective but far greater than needed for the task.

I do not claim to know who is a food addict and who isn't; my experience is that each person must decide for her or himself. But I'm on fairly firm ground when I say that the more serious one's weight problem is — in severity, duration, or combination thereof — the more appropriate it is to actively entertain the question.

➤ "Food addiction" is an awful term that may actually hinder acceptance of the phenomenon. People understand addiction to tobacco, or alcohol, or cocaine — a severe sensitivity to a substance that others handle in moderation. For those people, abstinence is a reliable "cure."

The principle of abnormal sensitivity pertains to food addicts too, but applying them is much more complicated. For example, with tobacco and the others, all forms are off-limits. But I can safely eat a piece of fruit, which is loaded with sugar, while I can't handle refinements such as table sugar. In another example, a number of substances that will lead me to overeat every time — peanuts, popcorn, and sugarless gum among them — can be taken in moderation by others who also call themselves food addicts.

And, of abstinence: If you don't touch food, you starve — a very severe cure indeed. But I apply the principle of abstinence nevertheless, moving the boundaries from "all or nothing" to "none of this, and clear limits on that." Some of my guidelines limit substances such refined sugar and flour. Others proscribe behaviors: The vast majority of time, for example, I determine my portions with a food scale and other measures. I'd rather not have to, but I am quite convinced that my "eye," when asked to determine an appropriate portion, is severely compromised — and probably broken forever.

Quite emphatically, I emphasize that these measures are for me, not for everyone. I believe all food addicts need limits, and that some of the limits will apply to many of us. But few of the food addicts I know follow the exact same guidelines.

Some of my boundaries were suggested; others I developed from painful experience. How many times did I have to try "just one" piece of gum, or just one handful of popcorn, to get it through my head that I just wasn't going to stop there?

As if these descriptions don't muddle the picture enough, there's plenty more: The term "food addiction" encompasses bulimia and anorexia, which I don't intend to cover extensively because they haven't been central to my eating problem. But I know, without doubt, that I have strong commonalities with both.

With bulimics, I share the tendency to binge eat. Their thing is to get rid of the load by vomiting, abusing laxatives, exercising obsessively, or other means. I haven't done those, yet, but I can relate to the dread and despair of what I've done to myself with food, yet again.

My tie to anorexics is that we're prone to controlling our experiences of the world via food. I do it by stuffing myself; they do it by proving they can tightly control their intake of food, if nothing else. I accept that we have strains of the same disease, even though I have a hard time imagining the day I'll get a charge out of not eating.

And still more: Some people are only refined-sugar addicts, or claim an even smaller set such as "chocoholics," but have no problem with flour or fat, for examples. At the other end of the range, I know people who have identified dozens of "trigger" foods that they must do without. Similarly, I know overeaters who also self-identify as anorexics or bulimics; I've met some who say they've been all three, having exhibited all tendencies at different times.

A hallmark of addicts' thinking is "all or nothing"; we like black and white far more than we like the grays. It is evident to me that around the question of addiction, the general populace has the same tendency: Addictions that can be clearly explained are easier to accept than ones with so many permutations. Variability makes the condition tougher for clinicians to study and to diagnose; for the rest of us, it is harder to differentiate when we're just indulging a bit too much from when we've crossed irrevocably into addiction.

PROBLEM EATER OR ADDICT; WHAT'S THE DIFFERENCE? In a word, choice. I began abusing substances other than food in junior high, beginning with cigarettes and eventually getting to marijuana and cocaine. I dabbled in alcohol, amphetamines, barbiturates, and acid, as well. Most people will have no problem accepting that every one of these substances is addictive; I sure don't, even while conceding that not everyone who uses these substances becomes an addict. Some take them in moderation, having fun when they do but not thinking about them otherwise. This can even be true of people who occasionally take too much of one of them.

I smoked cigarettes, up to 50 a day, for a dozen years. I smoked pot for 15 years, every day it was available. I started with cocaine in college, and before I quit, I was using the crack form often enough to skirt trouble at work.

I don't take any of those substances any more. I stopped cigarettes when Ronald Reagan doubled the federal cigarette tax. I stopped cocaine, when I finally realized that I would never, ever, get enough of it, no matter how much time, money, or attention I devoted to it. I stopped pot on no more impetus than a writing assignment I was given while in rehab.

In each case, I decided to stop. Even with cocaine, which many regard as especially habit-forming, I decided to stop — and then actually did! Addicts often "decide" to stop, but rarely try, or succeed if they do. Meanwhile, I've swore off food on many "morning afters," only to be back in the food by mid-morning. I have never been to "just eat less," not in the long term, not as a natural act. Unchecked, my eating will always expand, and so will my body, grotesquely. This is undeniable.

Some people are born with a predisposition to addiction, but anyone can develop it. It's not necessarily a linear process, and it's not inevitable once it's begun. But there is the point after which all choice is lost. I hear people talk about their "drug of choice," and I've known those, but with food, the correct phrase is "drug of no choice." I experienced that in a more easily illustrated way with cigars: For years, I was the type who bought a pack of five for a poker game and let three go stale in the glove box. Then, seemingly overnight, I wasn't: I'd become the type who was buying a box of 50 a week.

I can't tell you if you're an addict. But if you've been on lots of diets and just can't seem to keep to them, or to keep the weight off with any reliability, that might be a clue. Or, you can try some controlled eating: Buy a hot hoagie, or an ice cream cone, or whatever your current fave is. Take a few bites and then put it down. Walk away. Is it easy? Do you forget it's there? Or does it call out to you? Normal eaters can take it or leave it, just like normal drinkers can order a drink and then forget where they put it down. Addicts hardly ever forget like that.

INSURANCE-SUPPORTED REHAB SHOULD BE AS AVAILABLE TO FOOD ADDICTS AS TO OTHER ADDICTS. Rehab isn't a guarantee: Some addicts are beyond reach, others have to rehab more than once before they achieve stable recovery. But it has been the turning point for millions of addicts, over decades of treatment. It was for me: Even though I have used alternative residential treatment options since, that interlude was central to my new way of living.

Largely speaking, that option is not available to obese people today. It certainly isn't available to food addicts, since, of course, there is no medical-industrial-complex imprimatur for food addiction. Even if insurance companies wanted to extend this coverage to food addicts — and of course, they don't, because that will cost money — they would be hampered by the lack of accepted diagnostic standards. Of course, I didn't have the diagnosis of substance use disorder the day I entered South Oaks, even though I weighed in at 365 pounds. On the cusp of the managed-care era, I was approved as having obsessivecompulsive disorder, a diagnosis that was both accurate and dishonest, since no doctor had ever mentioned it until the hospital sought to get me approved.

I emphasize that I don't consider rehab to be a panacea. Among my acquaintances from that time, some got better and some didn't. As a rule, the expectation is that a third of rehab patients overcome their dependence. If that were to hold true to food addicts, it would make it the best treatment option by far.

IT DOESN'T HAVE TO TAKE 9 WEEKS; IT DOESN'T HAVE TO COST $50,000. Those were the parameters for my South Oaks stay, and that's in 1991 dollars. After managed care pulled the plug on hospital-based treatment, substitutes sprang up, including what I call itinerant rehab. The founders call it Acorn Food Dependency Recovery Services, based on the west coast of Florida. Instead of a bricks-and-mortar institution, their residential treatment is offered wherever a core of people want it; so far locales have included Massachusetts, New Jersey, Indiana, North Carolina, Maine and Florida.

Instead of the weeks-long tenures of most rehab stints, the longer Acorn events last five days, and last I heard, they're now working with a three-day model. And instead of being facilitated in hospitals with cadres of medical and support staff, they are most often held in rented private homes.

Even so, they felt like rehab to me, especially my first one, the only one I've attended in crisis. It took place in December 1999 just across the state line from Louisville. The years between South Oaks and southern Indiana were so much better than my life before, but as I looked back through journals in preparation for this book, I saw that I seldom went more than a few months in those eight years without a food mishap of some sort — a bad meal, a bad weekend, a bad vacation.

When I enrolled with Acorn, I was on a months-long bender that had resisted the actions that had pulled me back from the edge all those other times, and I'd finally admitted I wasn't getting better on my own.

It's worth noting that at my worst in that stretch, I maintained more than a 100-pound weight loss — that's a great illustration of how far the therapy, support groups, and South Oaks had brought me. But for the complex reasons of every human's condition, it became evident that more work remained for me.

Just like in Long Island, I got what I came for, a renewed appreciation for how serious my situation was, and a renewed willingness to seek and accept the help, support, and suggestions of others. Since then I've not sunk to such undependable abstinence again, and I've been more stable in most every other way as well.

In 1999, the five-day "intensive," as Acorn calls them, cost $1,500, meals and lodging included, plus another $350 for airfare, a night in a hotel, and other incidentals.

ANYONE CAN LOSE WEIGHT AND KEEP IT OFF. As with any large task, the issue is merely motivation, but despite the obvious stakes — from greater risks for heart disease and diabetes to joint pain and shortness of breath — most severely overweight people still view it as an inconvenience, rather than a threat.

If your house is on fire, you will race from the building, even jump from an upper-floor window if you have to. You're not going to think how inconvenient it is to have to rise from the easy chair in the middle of "Family Guy."

A better analogy might be a house whose timbers are under great stress, or whose poorly maintained mechanical systems are on the verge of giving out, and in that scenario, people have been known to just keep on getting by. As a teenager, I ruined an employer's truck engine by continuing to drive it after it had clearly broken down, so I understand the tendency.

But it cost $1,600 — yes, this was some time ago — to repair it, when if I'd just halted a half-mile earlier, it would have been maybe a couple hundred.

THE RELIABLE WAY OUT OF OBESITY IS VIA PERSONAL RESPONSIBILITY.
This point has been lost on the hundreds of folks who have railed against
my arguments for food addiction in periodicals, so I'm eager to make it
here: No one but me put the food in my mouth. Even if I had grown up imprisoned in a crawl space under the basement stairs (I wasn't), even if trag-
edy has befallen me every 15 minutes since (it hasn't), I'm still responsible
for what I eat. If my food is out of control (it was), then I'm responsible for
finding, requesting, and accepting the help I need.

I wasn't always so inclined. In childhood, I acquired and developed an attitude that nobody liked me and that the world was unfair, so I was forever
seeking someone who understood, and who would champion me. That's
just about the opposite of personal responsibility.

So how did I make such a leap? In about the last fashion I ever would have
expected.

**UNEQUIVOCALLY, DEPENDABLE RECOVERY HAS A SPIRITUAL COMPO-
NENT.** When I heard this, I balked. I pouted. I stalled. I wanted nothing to
do with religion, which I equated with spirituality. Another of my confu-
sions was that God was both a capricious asshole and a figment of human-
kind, a contradiction that would have required a God-like figure to pull off.

Those who put forth the spiritual idea were friends and advisers I'd met
at South Oaks, in some of the support groups I have attended, and on my
own. The phrasing they used was a "power greater than myself," which I was
certain was just a bullshit soft-pedaling of God.

When I examine it today, I see I should have been eager for it, considering that even though I'd long had great willpower, having lost more than a
hundred pounds several times, I'd always reached the day when that power
failed. A lack of power was precisely my problem.

I suggest that anyone who has dieted repeatedly but not kept the weight off
has a similar power deficit. Perhaps they too have felt they had the power
but hadn't exercised it well enough. But it wasn't until I finally took the suggestions to open my mind toward spirituality that the power to lose weight
and keep it off began to materialize.

You can think that's coincidence if you want, but as the closest witness to this phenomenon, I'll tell you I reached a different conclusion. And for skeptics, I'm pleased to report that religion had nothing to do with it and that I got to devise my own definition of what spirit meant to me; you can too. I just had to be willing to get out of the driver's seat.

Before getting on with the story, a few words about science:

I've done some reading on the current inquiries, and met many of the leading obesity researchers, including Mark Gold, Ernest Noble, Bart Hoebel, Serge Ahmed, Jeff Grimm, Rick Johnson, and Kelly Brownell. I respect and admire every one of them, and am thankful for their work.

I am very confident that eventually, establishment medicine and popular culture will accept both the existence of food addiction and its implications for severely overweight and obese people who haven't been able to change.

I'm quite clear that when that happens, it will have been largely influenced by what these researchers are doing, far more than the assertions I'm making based on my experiences and observations. This is patently obvious; I'm mentioning it to ensure readers that it is obvious to me, too.

I could have chosen to write chapter upon chapter about these interesting folks who are devoting their careers to the biggest public health threat of our time.

I may do that still, but it's not where I wanted to begin. The best contribution I can make to the effort is a personal story that I see as a counterpoint to the research. My intention is to persuade, and perhaps even to educate in a folksy way, but it is also a story of overcoming adversity.

I wouldn't be surprised if one of those researchers were to one day win a Nobel Prize for the research they're doing. But when I met them, at a private conference on obesity in Bainbridge Island, Wash., that gathered researchers, clinicians, counselors, and a few storytellers, I was surprised to observe that so many of them did not know any compulsive eaters.

I don't know whether to attribute that to the ivory tower, or if these personable, brilliant academicians merely reflect the broader population. I think most people don't recognize the compulsive eaters among us. Some are obese, but others aren't — there are anorexics and bulimics, for example, and I'm a compulsive eater too, even though I'm no longer obese. Not all obese people are compulsive, either.

But there are millions of us, and it would help everyone if you got to know us.

Nice to meet you.

2

Born To Eat

YOU DON'T HAVE TO HAVE AN ADDICT in your family history to become one, but it helps. The obvious one in mine was my mother's father.

Solly Goldberg was a warm, fascinating, and boisterous fellow who established a glass business in the shadow of the Depression that's still in the family today, employing about 135 people. He was a community leader on Boston's North Shore who inspired love and loyalty from family, friends, employees, and associates over decades.

But once he started drinking habitually, all he had built in mortar and reputation began to crumble. By the time he died — from liver failure in 1978 — his family had been irreparably sundered and his business was a brittle shell whose survival was in doubt.

At one time, the plan was for his son-in-law, my father Robert, to succeed him, and as his drinking worsened, the transition had begun, mostly by default. But in the early 1970s, a pig- headed row worsened by Solly's alcoholic lifestyle abruptly canceled that. Solly never stepped into our house after that, and his children never spoke civilly again.

Though it was my father who was suddenly unemployed, it was my mother, Joan, whose world was ruptured: Not only had the two most significant men in her life had a falling out, but Solly enlisted his only other child, my mother's sister Lois, to administer the business, forever sending him and their mother, Ruth, into her orbit and leaving my mother outside it.

At her core, my mother is proactive, and here she was, a front-row spectator to catastrophe. As catastrophes go, this was mild — no one was killed, no one was made homeless, and my dad soon started a competing business that exceeded Solly's in every way — but as my Mama Ruth would aphorize until her death three decades later, "When you stub your toe, it hurts you." My father's return to a strong business position was not mirrored domestically, and they ended their marriage within a few years.

It would be simplistic to blame the divorce on that one incident, and it would be facile to blame my food addiction on the undercurrents it left. It's true that my eating worsened during that time, but I'd had abnormal thoughts, and exhibited abnormal behaviors, around food long before.

I was called to food from the cradle. My mother recalls complaining to the family pediatrician that I just kept eating when my brother would have stopped. He assured her I would outgrow the proclivity, but that's one he just got wrong.

In my first food memory, I am perhaps 4. In the essential moment, my father enters the kitchen to discover me on the countertop, reaching into the upper cabinet where the ice cream cones were kept.

I am young enough that the story could have been cute, but for me it holds no warmth. I had fallen asleep and awakened to an empty house, and became convinced they'd gone off to get ice cream without me, so I had it coming.

It turned out that no one had gone for ice cream and I'd missed out on nothing. But the story's threads — of perceived unfairness and the primacy of food — have remained with me.

I can't think of any explanation for either stance. Home life was neither idyllic nor depraved, but was far closer to the former and well within the normal range. I was well provided for materially and grew up amid plenty of extended family. I showed fair promise in school and was encouraged to excel. Undeniably, among the fates of birth, I landed a pretty good one.

Family in the two generations before me was centered in Salem, Mass., site of the witch trials, although when I was 2 and my sister was on the way, my parents moved us to neighboring Marblehead, part flinty Yankee harbor, part blue-blood seaside community, and part burgeoning Boston suburb.

Proof of accomplishment came from both sides of the family. Although my father entered his in-law's business, his own father was also a success, in the leather business. Joseph Prager was a hero of his family, who had come before 5 of his 7 siblings from Eastern Europe and returned to bring the rest of the family to America.

Dad was the only surviving child, a bit lazy through school but talented once he applied himself, and so successful in his post-Solly endeavor that when he sold his business, it was a sum large enough sum to be reported in The Boston Globe. In addition to ability, his success was built on industry and iron will. I've never settled on whether he worked so hard because he was work-addicted, or if he just wanted to be out of the house.

I wasn't present for the early stages of my parents' relationship, of course, but it definitely degraded over time, and when they announced their divorce in 1983 — when we'd all gathered back in Massachusetts for a party to celebrate the marriage of my brother and his wife — the reaction among the siblings was "finally."

One way in which they were well matched, which may be more properly expressed as poorly matched, was in their drives to achieve, and while Dad could express his in business, Mom had only the rest of the world, and it was never quite big enough.

During the years we were growing up, she got a master's in education and eventually taught high school equivalency classes at a medium-security prison, right up until the day a plot to kidnap her was brought to light. She took her turn as president of the sisterhood at her temple, sang in a three-woman community-level performance troupe, and started Chart-a-Tour, which guided bus trips around Salem and Marblehead, whose historical claim is birthplace of America's Navy.

But her first management venue was the home, and unquestionably, our home reflected her more than the rest of us combined. If my father's compulsive tendency was work, my mother's was control. Dad never exercised a strong hand at home, but as the children became teens, he withdrew even his small stake and she annexed every inch of it.

These dynamics affected each of us differently. All three kids were bright, but my older brother, Rich, was chief achiever. He won the Latin prize of his senior class, reached French 5 as well, and even took Esperanto at the community college. (In his 50s, he's recently taken up Korean and Mandarin.) He has three college degrees: undergrad, in the classics, from Princeton, and graduate degrees from Wesleyan University and the New York State School of Forestry. He attended Outward Bound, the National Outdoor Leadership School, and walked the Appalachian Trail, from Georgia to Maine, on his own. He has climbed every peak in the Presidential Range in New Hampshire, and backpacked the world, the latter with his fiancée/wife (they married in Cyprus).

I'm proud of all he's done, although I certainly didn't like being the "other" Prager boy all through school. I understand today that he was driven by demons just like I was; it's just that, unlike mine, his pushed him toward results that society honors.

It is telling that I am able to report less about how it was for my sister, Judith, who also excelled academically. After a high school education she supplemented with religious studies, she achieved an architecture degree at Barnard. (Two out of three in the Ivy League! I was, indeed, the "other" one.)

By the time she graduated in 1981, she'd already designed a future not in architecture but in Israel, where she was called to make her life. It's as though we three were each given a normal dose of religion, but somehow Judy ended up with all three. Her brush with compulsion, if she had one, showed itself well into adulthood, when she developed an eating problem; it doesn't appear to be like mine.

As for myself, I offer two representations of my upbringing: The first is a line we used to toss around the family dinner table: We used to say that we needed a dog for Judy. My father had my mother to hassle, she had Rich, Rich had me, and Judy had no one.

Yes, that's an actual chuckle from the family archive.

The other comes from 1991, when, in a group therapy setting, I was asked to draw a scene of home life growing up. I did my best to place the windows proportionately and to get the flagstone walkway right, and the result wasn't too bad, considering my drawing deficiencies. But the first feedback I got from the others had nothing to do with the lines:

Where were the people?

I certainly didn't leave them out on purpose, but that's what open-ended exercises reveal. I was asked about my home and I drew a building, from an outsider's perspective.

With time to reflect, I've come to accept the picture as sad and accurate, if unexplained. Family anecdotes suggest I was naturally bright and sunny, outgoing and adventurous. One of my earliest memories is working the tables at my parents' club on bingo Sunday nights, approaching strangers and inviting myself to join them for repartee.

At home, we ate normally. Dinner was taken together, at a regular time, in the dining room. Some of our best memories came around that table, usually the result of my father's humor — before he stopped sharing it.

The food was neither awful nor awesome, but it was balanced, sensible, and occasionally suburban adventurous, such as my mother's treasureburgers, which had baked beans, a cocktail frank, or some other delectable leftover hidden inside.

The rest of the day was less regular, though certainly the family plan was for three meals a day. Breakfast was toast or an English muffin or a couple of Pop-Tarts, and lunch was either dispatched with us in the morning or purchased in the school cafeteria.

I ate what I was given, but unlike most of my classmates, I rarely was satisfied with that. I don't remember the first time I stole food, but I do remember the first time I was caught, at the Giant Valu in Salem. While my mother plied the aisles, I lurked up front, grabbing a piece of candy when I could and furtively eating it outside. I don't know how many I'd taken by the time the manager busted me, but I recall the shame I felt when he barred me from reentering.

Even so, the incident didn't scare me straight. It just made me eager not to be caught, and into my teens, I got a lot better at it.

I wasn't much of a saver when I was a kid, and when I came into cash, I knew where it would go. Some of the money came from generous relatives, but it also came from waitresses' tips that I scooped up before they cleaned up, or more significantly, from the envelopes my mother used for the household accounts.

In my early teens, I was taking 10 bucks at a crack, which was not insignificant money in the early '70s. Eventually, my mother started noticing. I remember her complaining that money was disappearing, and she once said she suspected that one of the neighborhood kids knew about the envelopes and was entering via our unlocked back door.

It seems unfathomable, now, but I recall wondering which kid it was. I knew where I was getting my money, but I somehow didn't connect that information with the fact that her money was disappearing. I thought that she was making it up, or that someone from outside really was coming in.

I used the money, as often as not, at Lena's sub shop. I didn't make a list in those days because I was only buying one sub before I headed home to dinner, and it didn't occur to me that the clerk was taking note of me.

Turns out he was, and one day while my mother was looking for me, she met up with him. I must have asked her to pick me up there and then started walking home; I'm not sure. When she caught up with me, she confronted the issue immediately: "He told me you come in practically every day. Is that true?"

"No," I lied. "I don't have the money." Incredibly, she said she believed me, which is now my symbol for the power of denial. Here I was, 14 or 15 years old and probably around 250 pounds. Clearly I was getting a lot more food than my brother or sister, and she'd just been told by a neutral source that I visited his sandwich shop every day.

"Good," she said. "That was my first question, how you could afford it." We didn't discuss it again for 19 years.

In high school, I got a job at the superette around the corner. I didn't apply with intent to steal; I was just a teenager looking for part-time work. Pretty soon, though, I was hitting the freezer for ice cream sandwiches during my shift, and taking home a small bag of junk food — Beefaroni, a pint of ice cream, Cheese Nips, whatever — after closing.

The subject of money came up around that stuff too, but she never delved deeply and disapprovingly accepted that I was "pissing away" my minimum wages on junk food. The truth is that not only was I hitting the shelves, I was pocketing money from the register to pay for food elsewhere, to finance my poker playing, and other essentials.

Early photos of me show a pudginess but no worse, and I recall neither body shame nor many adjustment issues early on, but I do recall the hubbub that rippled across the third grade when, during gradewide cursory health evaluations, the nurse recited for a note taker that I weighed 132 pounds. It was embarrassing, and yet it barely compared to a few days later, when a postcard arrived from school announcing the extent of my abnormality.

"Do they think I don't know you're overweight?" my mother shouted. I see now that she was probably frustrated by what was happening with me, and embarrassed by her "failure" to bring me up "right," but at the time, I wasn't nearly as sanguine.

My first diet didn't stem from that incident, but it came soon enough. My mother prescribed the Stillman Diet, whose secret ingredient was water: Drink eight 8-ounce glasses of water a day and you'll be less likely to over-eat. She put eight toothpicks on the left side of the sink, and I was to move one to the right with every tumblerful. I don't recall ever moving all eight.

I was introduced to therapy around the same time, the fall of fourth grade. That summer, I'd gone to Alton, an overnight camp on Lake Winnipesaukee in New Hampshire, and camp fathers had advised my parents that I was an unhappy boy who needed help.

Every other Wednesday into the spring of 1967, my mother and I would drive into Boston's Back Bay for my therapy, but if it accomplished anything, I'm unaware of it. The only feedback my mother recalls from the therapist is that I spoke of "a fire inside." All I remember is that I always lied to him, trying to prove I was OK rather than trying to learn why I wasn't.

Over the next three summers, Alton continued as the hothouse for my social fumbling, and by the last one, I'd reached the nadir of Alton life: During its all-day Flag Rush, the revered culmination of the camp's season-long color war, I was assigned to the woods. While almost everyone else was striving for honor on the field of battle, I was given a whistle and assigned to disappear. Officially, woodsmen were charged with raising an alarm if invaders tried to sneak onto our territory for attack, but everyone knew you got assigned to the woods for being a loser.

The final twist of my Alton struggles played out for years after I'd left: My first cousin, Larry, went there and blazed a trail as successful as mine was shamed: He not only never ended up in the woods, he was a popular camper who became a popular counselor, reaching the top rung of camp leadership.

In the winter of 1970, meanwhile, my parents concluded that they needed more than fun and games for their son's summer and signed me up for Tahoe, a camp in upstate New York designed for fat kids. I've always expressed resentment of having not been consulted, but the reality is that I would not have cooperated had they asked. The wintry night that two of the camp's directors came to the house to interview me, I blustered that I wouldn't go at all, or would run away upon arrival.

My vehemence had two parts: Not only did I want to return to Alton, I desperately wanted not to be lumped in with a bunch of fat kids. My commitment to Alton remains my strongest proof of how strongly I can cling to habits that aren't working for me.

I never did have the courage to run, though my second summer there, I vaguely recall more than one off-limits excursion to find a store whispered in camper lore, a place where you could buy all the things they didn't serve in the dining hall. I did find it eventually, but if I bought anything, it was cigarettes, not food.

Controlling intake was half of the Tahoe formula: three meals a day, doled out under watchful eyes. The highlight was the Sunday breakfast of waffles and reduced-sugar syrup, but even that was sullied by the weekly weigh-in that preceded it. The entire camp lined up to be quantified, recorded, and if necessary, cajoled for not working hard enough.

I did come to like Tahoe for the other half, which was constant sports activity. At home I'd been the fat kid chosen last for every team; here, I was one of the better athletes. Perhaps that's why I willingly returned the second summer and then followed the four men who'd run Tahoe when they broke away to start their own camp, Kingsmont, in Western Massachusetts.

I did lose weight in those three summers, more each time than the summer before, but only because I'd returned each time at a new top, having recovered the weight I'd lost and found even more. Not only was it a summer-only regimen, but it addressed only intake and activity, and then as today, that's too simplistic for most out-of-kilter eaters, especially those who landed at fat camp.

I don't recall education being part of the curriculum, but what were they going to teach me, anyway? Calorie charts? Good nutrition? Even if I didn't know that stuff, it wasn't my ignorance of them that was making me fat.

So what was? I don't have much of an answer, but disaffection and alienation were central to my personality — even more so than usual for a teen. Between 7th and 8th grades I started smoking, in part because it gave me entrée to the other illicit smokers.

A couple years later, I "joined" a group of borderline young citizens who congregated at a gas station near the high school, where I wasn't liked but was allowed to stay. That affiliation led to an invitation to join the Okommakamesit Veteran Firemen's Association, an old-town Marblehead fellowship that took its hand-pump fire tub to musters in New England and New York to see who could spray water the farthest and most accurately. Any joy I might have felt at being included was short-circuited when I found out why: They needed heft at the hosehead to help point the nozzle.

The station proprietor was a jolly, middle-aged ne'er-do-well named Cecil who enjoyed the company of teenagers. I pumped gas for no wages and otherwise tried to justify my existence while others sat around, drank beers below window level, and shot the shit.

The more I hung out there, the more my parents objected, and in one of our confrontations over it, theyinformed me that Cecil had a criminal record and that police suspected illegal activity was going down at the station. But just about the worst transgression I ever saw there was the sale of a nickel bag of pot.

But they were oblivious to the clumsy, white-collar criminal conspiracy that was taking shape just about then: I know about it because I devised it and then, with Cecil's grateful support, carried it out. Cecil hadn't been filing the daily sales reports that the home office expected, and eventually, they told him to document his business or to get out.

Abruptly, it appeared I'd be back on the street, socially speaking, so I swept into action. Cecil had a bottom line figure for daily sales, and I set about concocting post-dated reports that at least got close to that number. When my "office hours" proved too short for the task, I took the adding machine and daily-report forms home to work into the night.

You have to be wondering: Why would a 17-year-old eagerly spend hours bent over an adding machine, committing fraud for free? My addled reasoning, which I've seen enough times since to easily recognize, was that I wanted to be liked, and if I couldn't win favor by who I was, maybe I could by what I did.

I don't know how much I hoped to gain with Cecil, who liked me fine as far as it went – I'd always done better with adults than with contemporaries. But I imagine I fancied myself the potential hero if I could save our clubhouse.

I can assure you, the other denizens weren't thinking anything of the kind: Some were unconcerned, some were oblivious, and others were spending their energies on dating and mating.

I would have been doing that too, if only. But I never fit into an arena less than I did into dating. I was malformed around girls for as long as I remember, certainly before my body began to mirror my distortion.

My understanding today is that it's fairly common for kids to go through a stage playing "doctor," which suggests there was at least a moment in time when I was in the mainstream. But for me, that stage never closed. Long after the girls I approached made clear they'd moved on, I was still asking.

One thread that spooled out from that beginning is that I grew not just familiar with rejection from the girls I wanted to play with, but to expect the hammer. Perhaps, with a knowing adviser or just a few more smarts, I might have grasped the notions that friendship precedes intimacy, that baldly asking for sex rarely works, that expecting failure is the best way to invite it — but I didn't clue into those for another couple of decades.

Another thread that developed was the ill-serving connection that sex – not friendship, nor closeness, nor partnership — was the sole goal of intimacy. From well before puberty but then right on into it, I was not so much a suitor as a lecher, and a fat, awkward lecher at that.

Though I'm quite aware that the fat wasn't the core of my problems, it sure didn't help me move smoothly through the world. People are averse to fatties, and at no time is that more acute or overt than during adolescence. I still sting over the incident in 7th grade that cemented this knowledge in me.

Boys and girls typically took gym class on opposite sides of a partition, but when the curriculum called for square dancing, the wall was folded back. The only touching was hand to hand, but one of my partners was moved, when paired with me, to pull her hand inside her sleeve, so she wouldn't actually have to touch me.

We never spoke about it, of course — I don't even know who she was — but I have never doubted she was recoiling not only from my body but from my soul. The experience helped solidify my belief that just being fat was enough to be excluded from the mainstream in public and painful ways.

I also know that the same girl could have done the same thing with another boy and he would have shrugged it off, if not in the moment then in a day or a week. My involvement in the episode has been to keep this faceless girl alive in memory for more than 35 years, so shamed that until now, I've never shared the story.

Even among the kids who wouldn't just have shrugged it off on their own, I can't help but think that many of them would have had someone to ask for help, a father or brother or someone, to share the pain if not to get helpful advice, but I didn't. I have no way of knowing if that was my father's deficiency, or my brother's, or mine; almost certainly, it was a family condition. Regardless, the event resonates not only because of the girl, but because of the loneliness and cluelessness it exemplifies.

The fact is, although the slights of girls cut deeper, I wasn't doing too hot with the guys, either. On one of my first days at the junior high, I remember alienating a group of cool guys just by telling them how excited I was to be hanging with them, since I wasn't used to it. (Translation: "You're talking to a loser.")

In junior high and high school, I followed three crossing routes: trying to fit in, trying to stand out, and trying to disappear. I fared worst at fitting in, but did achieve minor notoriety on several fronts.

When we returned from our holiday vacation to France and England midway through sophomore year, I started wearing the bowler I had purchased on Portobello Road in London wherever I went, much to the consternation of Mr. Russell, an old-school teacher who believed it discourteous to wear hats indoors. But I became recognizable not just as the fat kid, but the fat kid who wore the odd hat.

That trip left its mark not only on top of my head, though; incidents in Paris and London a few days apart left their scars inside it. The second incident, in which a male reveler kissed me in Trafalgar Square at midnight on New Year's Eve, probably wouldn't have been a big deal if the first one hadn't still been clawing at me.

I'd been on a bench at the entrance of the Louvre, waiting for my family to come out, when I was accosted by an amorous Parisian who thought I was a girl. He was on me quickly, and he kissed me repeatedly before I could sputter "garcon, garcon" — which I've always thought was impressively multilingual under the circumstances. He paused, looked me over again, and jauntily dismissed me without so much as a c'est la vie before moving on.

I don't recall what I told my family when they came out, but the incident, later bolstered by my Waterloo at Trafalgar, opened new vistas in my shame. To my generalized body loathing, I added a specific indictment of my breasts, which had become more prominent than many of my female classmates could claim.

I took to wearing my overcoat through the school day, and in fall and spring, I wore a grimy blue windbreaker on even the warmest days. The only concession I made to summer was to wear short sleeves. Even though I liked to swim, I would either decline to go in or I would wear a t-shirt, which not only was a lousy strategy for blending in, but when I'd exit the pool, I'd become the winner, or loser, of my own wet T-shirt contest.

I especially hated communal shower rooms. In junior high, they were the crowning humiliation of gym class. Although I was once a Little League All-Star (scouting report: "Hits a ton, weighs a ton"), I couldn't keep up with my peers athletically. But even if I could have, even if some coach had wanted me to come out for football because I could clog the line, I doubt whether I would have because it would have meant daily showers with the boys.

(In the freshman dorm at college, we had no private showers, so I used the one we had sparingly. I preferred not bathing, even though my stink led to more estrangement and unwanted notoriety. Some guys wanted nothing to do with me, and even my friends made rules about when I could sit on their beds. And still I valued covering up more.)

Though it feels like I was known only for my gross anatomy, I did, in fact, also stand out for nonphysical reasons: In my junior and senior years I was public address announcer for our football games, and one of those years, I read announcements over the school loudspeaker every afternoon as well. For a couple of seasons I was also manager of the school soccer and baseball teams, until one coach caught me smoking behind the grandstand and told me not to come back.

When I collect it all on a page like this, my first reaction is, how I can claim

I was a nonentity during those years when, for example, the entire high school heard me on the intercom every afternoon at 2?

The answer is that despite such facts, I never felt a part of the student community. No doubt, had that group therapy assignment been to draw a scene from high school life, I would have done my best to align the bricks on the façade. I was growing up apart from everyone around me, lonely in whatever group I was in.

Undoubtedly, the separation wasn't a figment — at my 30th high school reunion, three classmates expressed sorrow to me for how I was ostracized — but my perception of it was worse than reality.

Meanwhile, I was certain that all my maladjustment rested in my flab, which at the turn of 1974 had me well over 300 pounds. With the help of a family friend and under the direction of one of the most famous diet gurus ever, I was about to find out how wrong I was.

3

A Diet, Not a Solution

IN THE FALL AND WINTER of 1973, some of my junior-class mates were pulling lobster pots, some were playing sports, some were having sex with each other before their parents got home.

Partly because I was tolerated more by adults than peers, and partly because of the free doughnuts, I was again volunteering for my congressman, Michael J. Harrington, this time in a three- or four-staffer campaign-finance office in which I was the sole volunteer. I was also there because Ernie Weiss, a longtime family friend, was the executive in charge. He was a sympathetic guy who sometimes would return me home in his exotic French sports car.

One day on the way home, he asked me if I'd consider consulting with a doctor he'd been seeing for weight control. I was surprised by this, since he never struck me as having a weight issue, but I said yes. The doctor was in New York, he said, but he would take me to the airport, fly with me, and escort me into the first visit. I would actually get a day off from school, to jet down to the big city for the day. (On my third or fourth visit, I caught 7 innings of a Sox-Yankees game before having to catch my plane home.)

I also liked that it was an opportunity to be special. Not only would the jetting-down-to-New York thing work for that, he said that if I tried to get an appointment with this guy on my own, it would take me more than a year, but he could get me in.

The doctor's name was Robert G. Atkins, and his Diet Revolution was just taking hold.

On that first visit, I weighed in at 332½, meaning that I had, on average, added 20 pounds onto my body for every year of my life. Owing to a glucose-tolerance test, the visit lasted 7 hours, filled mostly by peeing in a cup or waiting for the next time to pee in a cup, but it did include an audience with the doc.

I was unimpressed.

What sticks out most from the interview was when he asked me if I wasn't bothered to be missing out on so much, such as sunning myself on the beach at Saint Tropez. In France. On the French Riviera. Literally, he was trying to motivate a 300-pound-plus 16-year-old suburbanite by suggesting that when I lost my weight, I would find myself among the beautiful people in the south of France.

I suppose he'd honed the pitch for his patients from his East Side neighborhood, but as a diet doctor, he certainly should have known that one size does not fit all. After a bit more of his diet-pop psychology, I asked him if I was supposed to be feeling regretful for having gotten myself into such sorry shape.

"Never mind what you're supposed to be feeling," he thundered, scaring me. "Just answer the question!"

Clearly, we weren't going to be buddies, but his regimen kept me coming back. At my two-week weigh-in, I'd lost 30 pounds — yes, 2 per day — and I would drop about a hundred more before my willpower would peter out.

Why, when I'd never lost any appreciable weight outside of summer boot camp, was I able to do this, especially when my only impetus was special circumstance and the solicitude of a family friend?

First, those conditions aren't to be discounted: Until then, I'd had scant claim to specialdom, and most of it had been of the bad kind: The year I made the top rung of Little League, none of the uniforms in the team's box fit me, so a league representative took me shopping. All season, I stood out both for my size and for the much larger scarlet number emblazoned on my back.

But also, it was a plan that rewarded black-and-white thinking. Instead of balance, there was the "right" stuff — protein and fat — and the "wrong" stuff — fruit and vegetables. And though I didn't know it then, and I wouldn't have related the knowledge to myself if I did, black-and-white thinking is a hallmark of addictive behavior.

And probably most significant of all, the Atkins diet capitalizes on four of the sweetest words in a problem eater's world:

All.

You.

Can.

Eat.

Most people who are overweight aren't that way because they make poor substance choices, though they usually do. It's because they eat too much. For me, certainly, barring some foods for the right to binge on the rest was a deal I could live with.

It was only gravy, so to speak, that the approved list included whipped cream and bacon-and-cheese soufflés. When I'd go out to eat with my family, I'd order a steak and not much more, but for dessert I'd get to order another steak. At home, I learned to cook, specializing in six-egg omelettes bathed in butter and "smoothed out" with heavy cream. If I was making Hebrew Nationals, I would munch on a cold one while I fried up a few more. Cheese was my oyster.

Unfortunately, I had the self-awareness of a typical teenager and understood none of the dynamics. I thought I had the secret and would be able to stay on this path eternally. I thought people's admiration — and more importantly, their sharing it with me — would last forever. I thought my willpower, even under the relatively easy circumstances, would last forever.

Forever turned out to last about 18 months.

Assuredly, it was an excellent time to become more socially acceptable, As the weight receded, I spent a semester working for Harrington in Washington, returned for the flurry of farewell senior-class activities, and did a summer of paid constituent-services work in the district.

In some ways, I was pretty hot stuff, but in the most important way, I still wasn't. In the first months, I was losing weight but was still fat, so I could hardly complain that I wasn't dating. But as my body shrank and my social life didn't swell, my resentments did.

My mistake was that as I got closer to normal size, I thought I was getting closer to normal.

With more awareness, I might have learned the first fact of fat — that fat isn't the problem. It is **a** problem, but even more troubling was my stew of personality flaws, maladjustments, and misconceptions that would require years of therapy and other tactics to uncover, accept, and address. The weight was both an effect of these conditions and a contributor to them. When I lost it, what I really lost was my layer of explanation.

What I gained, meanwhile, was a new way of eating. When I was following the good-food/bad-food routine, eating as much as I wanted was a harmless curiosity. As I lost the ability to stay within those lines, however, it became mere binge eating. It might be unfair to say that Dr. Atkins made me a binge eater because I was leaning that way when we met. But his plan certainly solidified the habit.

By the time I left for Ohio University that fall, my Atkins mojo was already in retreat — and then my supply lines changed dramatically. I went from having steak with my steak to whatever protein the cafeteria marms would dole out, once I'd won permission for individual treatment. Most often it was a hunk of chicken breast, pressure-cooked into institutional pallor, or perhaps a hunk of unadorned tuna from an industrial-sized can.

To obtain it, I had to interrupt someone from their duties at every meal, so second helpings seemed an imposition, especially since I was supposed to be the diet guy. It wasn't long before I was banging my fist on snack bars all over town, and the fabled "freshman 15" became, for me, the freshman 50.

For a while, I clung to the illusion that I was still dieting, but when I finally admitted the charade, I also starting drinking alcohol again. By spring, I'd also given in to marijuana, which theretofore I had shunned, resolutely and puritanically; if the subject came up as my pals puffed, I huffed about how they'd never get me to do that stuff. It would have been one thing if I'd tried it and decided it wasn't for me, but it was just closed-minded bluster.

Today I can say that I've tried it and it's not for me – but I needed 15 years to discover that it wasn't, and in that time, I smoked it practically every day that I had it – on planes, at games, and on the way to my grandfather's funeral. During that time, I eventually tried almost every drug out there — I drew the line at heroin, resolutely and puritanically — and even took to selling several of them, mostly just to finance my habits.

When I left college, I hadn't yet returned to my top weight, but I was substantially larger, and I'd wasted my four years in at least two significant ways. Not by much, but the lesser of the two was sex, which was practically a requisite of campus life in mid-'70s Athens, Ohio. I did manage to lose my virginity before I left town, but only barely.

That still feels like a loss, but the other one — the whole education thing — was worse. I attended only some of my classes, only some of the time, and left college with a 2.4 grade-point average — the same weak, middling, beneath-my-ability ground I'd occupied in high school.

Worse, through obstinance and indolence, I left without a degree. In my last semester, I thought one teacher was a bonehead and couldn't bear to listen to his drivel, so I just handed in the assignments, a tactic I'd employed before. That was acceptable behavior to some teachers, but he'd made clear it wouldn't be acceptable to him, and just as he'd promised, he flunked me for nonattendance. That would have been enough to scuttle my graduation bid, but I stopped attending another course in the sixth week, was unable to pull off the final, and failed that one too. They were the only two courses I failed in the four years.

The way it worked at Ohio U., one applied for graduation — and attended commencement — before grades were in. Though I knew I needed not one miracle but two, I didn't confide the circumstances to my family members who came to celebrate my "achievement." The timing was enough to enable denial, but my next steps imply that I would have lied no matter what.

First, my parents bought me a car as a graduation gift and I accepted it, even though I knew before I'd driven a mile that the miracles hadn't materialized. Then, I followed that up by issuing resumes that said I had a bachelor's in journalism, a degree I didn't actually gain until 5 years later.

When I moved north in my fraudulently gained auto, to begin my fraudulently gained job as a reporter at the 17,000-circulation Painesville (Ohio) Telegraph, it was on the same situationally (un)ethical ground I'd been treading all my life, with an appetite that was still seeking its limit.

The car also carried my eating to another level. I could now buy more from the grocery store than what I could carry, and my restaurant choices weren't limited to walking distance.

In fact, I didn't walk anywhere anymore, not even to the McDonald's at the end of my street. Soon my little Datsun 310 was revealing plenty about me: My back seat was filled with empty fast-food wrappers, sacks, and cups, and the car itself was listing toward the driver's side, not from the wrappers but from what their former contents were doing to me.

More often than grocery stores and drive-thrus, though, I frequented convenience stores, which reached just the right spot in my addict brain:

➤ They are ubiquitous, which means a fix is never far away.

➤ Unless someone is in line in front of you, the gratification is instant.

➤ They are stocked disproportionately with junk food.

➤ They have high staff turnover, which means you are less likely to experience the disdain in the eyes of your dealer.

When I was assigned to a night shift to help produce a morning edition of the paper that would be edited in Painesville but assembled 20 miles away, it institutionalized two eating sessions into every working day.

I'd graze at a low level on the way to the paste-up shop, perhaps getting a couple extra bags of chips when I stopped for the takeout dinner I'd eat at my desk. It was as close to controlled eating as I got; I found that if I dived in too deeply, I would not only be uncomfortable in my desk chair, but I would be unable to concentrate on the work to be done. So I indulged in the food equivalent of the three-martini lunch, enough to take the edge off without going over it.

But the buy for the ride back home was different. We'd be done by 11 or so, and I'd indulge in the relief of knowing that I owed the world no more that day and could now eat with abandon.

Before the ride home, which I'd share with Larry King when he was the Mutual Radio Network's overnight man, I'd stop at one of the mini-marts on Route 20 in search of two types of food: For the road, I wanted nothing that needed heating or assembling, and enough of it to last the 30-minute journey. But I also needed enough to get me through to morning without having to go out again.

Under these conditions, my weight completed its comeback from the first Atkins foray and set out for new heights. I have no way of knowing how high I got, or how high I would have gotten had my supervisor not suggested in December 1980 that I visit a pal of his, a leading editor at The Evening Times in West Palm Beach, Fla., while on vacation at my parents' winter home in Delray Beach.

The pal had been supplanted, but his replacement anticipated an opening due to an upcoming retirement, and I returned to Ohio galvanized for my move south: I'd be living in a beachfront condo in a land of bathing suits and T-shirts, and I didn't relish having to cover up all the time.

Thus began my second Atkins effort, although this time without the doctor's direct input, and I was well on the way down the scale when I moved in May. I felt like a lottery winner: Not only had I traded winter on Lake Erie for endless summer on the Atlantic, but I was now living rent-free in my parents' place, the nicest home I'd ever have: a top-floor, two-bedroom aerie with ocean and Intracoastal Waterway views. Instead of saving what would have been my rent, I bought a completely inappropriate sports car.

I joined a gym for the first time, developed a passable social life among my colleagues, and even had sex a few times, albeit with neither intimacy nor fulfillment.

Even though all the changes were just as superficial as they'd been in high school, I again concluded my problems were solved. I was so sure, I decided to have breast-reduction surgery to tidy up what had always been my bitterest bane: my man tits.

I suppose people with super big hips hate their super big hips, and those with big bellies hate their big bellies. At 300-plus pounds, none of my parts were exactly slender, but my breasts were easily my most outsized parts, and oh, did I hate them.

Being fat was bad, but being of semi-indeterminant gender — "Pat"-like, to "Saturday Night Live" fans — was mortifying. I blamed my tits for the incidents at the Louvre and in Trafalgar Square, and they were why I always wore at least one more layer than climate called for, no matter how much more it made me sweat — as if fat guys didn't sweat enough already.

Now that I was "cured," I was determined to have them removed, even when I learned that the surgery would cost $2,500. Even if I was living rent-free, that was still eight weeks' pay. I asked my insurer to cover it but expected to be denied — in their position, I sure would have said no — so I also petitioned my dad, either as funder or lender. I told him I was going to do it under any circumstances, but that I would appreciate help.

His only question was, what happens if you gain the weight back? Offended by the implication, I told him I didn't need to know because I was never going back.

I never learned what he would have done because, incredibly, the insurance company acceded. Turns out there's another name for man boobs, gynecomastia, and it was a coverable condition.

It also turned out that my dad was right: I should have asked what could happen if I gained the weight back, not only on general principle, but because I did eventually gain it back. Again. And then some. Again.

The answer was that as I gained, my breasts did begin to reinflate, but more in proportion to the rest of me, so never again were they the freakish beacons of my youth. But even the operation, on top of the condo, and the car, and the rest, did not bring happiness. I understood vaguely that these were shallow, external factors, but I thought that they should have at least brought me exciting-if-shallow thrills, which at that time I was willing to settle for.

Before too long, I decided that my alienation was Florida's fault and that I should relocate; in some circles, that's known as a geographical cure. I was so gleeful to go that I hit my horn long and hard when I hit the Georgia line. It would take me a decade to stop blaming the place, and another decade to grasp that the only place I could find happiness was inside myself.

The destination this time was back to Massachusetts, under circumstances not dissimilar to how I ended up in Florida — I went to visit family and stopped in at the local paper. This time it was The Evening News, the Salem daily that had been the family's hometown newspaper since before I was born. I had interned there in 1978, and decided to visit Rollie Corneau, who'd been my bureau chief that summer and who was now city editor.

The occasion for my visit was the wedding party for my brother, Rich, and his new wife, Beverly, the one around which my parents announced they were divorcing. The pat answer I developed for why I took such a lateral move — from a small afternoon paper in West Palm Beach to a small afternoon paper in Salem, where I would have to pay rent again, no less — was that I wanted to support my family, or more specifically, my mother, whom I thought would need at least one of her children around while she went through the dissolution.

But my real motivation was, as usual, selfish. I thought I would fit in better back in the Northeast, working at the paper that had published my birth announcement. I did feel less alien, if only because I knew the streets and recognized the seasons, but I soon learned that, indeed, you can't go home again.

For instance, I reassembled the poker gang I'd played with during high school, but at the first game, we dealt more lines of cocaine than hands of cards, and after that, we dispensed with the cards altogether. Soon, we moved on to cooking and smoking it in its new-fangled, intensified form, crack.

I'd used coke off and on since college, but had fairly well contained it to the occasional Saturday night. But now, any night had party potential. Old pals led to new acquaintances, including one or two unsavory ones.

One night, my friend Oscar, whose drug use had led him to drop out of the medical profession and to let his driver's license lapse, asked me to drive him into Cambridge and, after he got permission from his pal "Banny," invited me up. For four or five mostly uninterrupted hours, we stood in the apartment's small kitchen taking turns leaning over a spoon kept red-hot by an electric burner. Alternately, we would pass a paper cone, drop a rock of coke onto the spoon's tiny bowl, and inhale as the drug vaporized.

I say "mostly uninterrupted" because at one point, I was ordered to leave because "the Colombians" were coming to deliver more coke, and they only dealt with people they knew.

Within a month or so, Banny had fled his Cambridge apartment — or was it the Colombians? — and moved into Oscar's seaside rental, just a couple blocks from my place. Though I began spending too many evenings and essentially all my disposable cash over there, events I witnessed let me think that my use wasn't as serious as that of my friends.

Banny brought his paranoia north with him, for example, and more than once I witnessed him shouting menacingly into a kitchen light fixture, threatening either the dealers or the police, who he thought had bugged the place.

And while I was never unable to pay my rent, Oscar continued to separate from the grid, figuratively and literally. When nonpayment led to his electricity being cut off, his landlord downstairs allowed him to run an extension cord up the stairs — in exchange for some blow. Oscar used it to connect a lamp and a hot pot so he could see as he cooked his coke.

There was one other notable way in which I was different not only from these two, but from the other ex-poker pals with whom I hovered, hoping to catch a free pop or two. Apart from occasional shots of sugar — Banny and Oscar favored Emack and Bolio's premium ice cream — most frequent cocaine users lose the desire to eat, and Banny and Oscar grew thinner by the month.

Though I commented bitterly that I had to be the only cokehound on the planet whose weight went up, I refused to let my dalliance impinge on my true drug: I would force the food down when the coke in my system urged otherwise, or I would put the pipe down before it got the chance to.

Though my Atkins willpower had survived the move north better that it had when I went away to college, I was maintaining my weight more from the gym habit I'd also brought with me than from my food plan. Eventually, I was joining the boys on E&B runs, and then I started reacquainting myself with Stone's Bakery, at the end of my block, where my family had sometimes shopped when I was a youngster.

Party nights began colliding with working mornings, which is unavoidable when your shift starts at 5 a.m. Too often, I arrived on perhaps an hour's sleep — or the pretense thereof.

I'd started successfully at the News, assigned to edit a new section front. So I was pretty shocked when my boss pulled me aside a few months later and told me that my work had become the most in need of correction on the production floor. "I don't know what's wrong," he said, "but you'd better fix it."

The problem, of course, was my escalating drug abuse, for which I blamed where I was and whom I was with. I hadn't yet heard the adage, "Wherever you go, there you are," and I hadn't otherwise figured out that the constant in all these places was me. So I moved again.

This time, I chose Hartford, substituting family-visit happenstance for a career plan for yet a third time. Three months into my Salem stint, I'd gone to Connecticut to visit Rich and Bev, whom I knew hardly at all. Everyone else in the family had gone to Cyprus for the wedding, but she and I hadn't met until the reception, months later.

Passing through Hartford, I was impressed that it had grown a skyline, and

I already thought well of its newspaper, the Hartford Courant.. Its reputation was bigger than its circulation — and its circulation was roughly four times those of my first three papers combined. Connecticut might be a small pond, but the Courant was by far its biggest fish, and I'd had yet to work at a big fish. So I applied.

When I reported for work the week before Labor Day, I was beginning my fourth newspaper job in just over five years. It would be incorrect to say that I couldn't hold a job, but much more of that behavior and I would have qualified as a "journalistic saddle tramp," as a boss in West Palm Beach had described himself.

Thankfully, though, Hartford is where I stopped running away. When I left 9 years later, I would be vastly changed, not only in body size but, for the first time, inwardly. But before I could begin that ascent, I had more descending to do, and I got right to it.

Moving to a new state is uprooting for anyone. So is shifting from an early-morning schedule to the night side, and I attempted both simultaneously without even considering the consequences. And then I supercharged my dislocation by taking well more than a month to find and then settle into an apartment.

By then, I'd settled into a routine similar to Painesville nights: Stop at one of the few places open on the way home and load up on enough food to get me through to morning. Only on the roughest nights would I meet the dawn, but I would often fall asleep on the couch, lights and TV ablaze, and wake up in the bedroom without remembering how I'd gotten there.

Typically I would rise in early afternoon and not eat until I got to work, if only because I remained full from the night before. That made the first couple of hours at work my sharpest; once I ate, my thinking would be divided hopelessly between grammar and gluttony: What might I eat next? Could I hit the vending machine again without being noticed? Where might I stop on the way home?

In addition to inconsistency of editing, the flow of food sometimes brought inconsistency of mood, though not so I was able to notice a connection. Partly this was because I ate so irregularly that it was difficult to draw conclusions. Partly it was because the links between blood sugar and mood, now well accepted, weren't so well known. And partly it could have been because there's another word for moodiness — childishness — so who needed a more nuanced explanation?

Regardless, it was something many colleagues knew: I could be bright and sunshiny, or I could be dark enough to suck all the lightness from a room. You never knew when you approached: Which version would you get? Such capriciousness was easily the worst facet of what I brought to the workplace, and undercut whatever skills I showed.

In an alternate scenario, my superiors could easily have treated me as just an unreliable employee and acted accordingly, denying me advancement if not worse. Instead, one of them, Ed Lafreniere, reached out to me as an individual instead of just as an underling. He called me into his office and suggested I consider seeking therapy.

He told me he had done it and it had helped him and many others in the newspaper business; perhaps, he said, it could help me. I have no clue whether it was providence or coincidence that I was willing that day to listen, but when he told me about the company's employee assistance program, I not only made an appointment, I kept it.

After some discussion, the counselor suggested rehab, and at first, I said OK; I even started making inquiries with my bosses about going away. They were unstintingly supportive, and by the time I returned for a second session with the EAP counselor, I was getting used to the idea.

But then she told me rehab would use the 12 Steps, the recovery regimen worked out by the founders of Alcoholics Anonymous in the 1930s and since adapted by dozens of other groups and by many treatment centers. When I heard that one of the early steps would require me to acknowledge God (not exactly accurate, but that's what I heard), I called a halt right there.

Sure, I might have to make some changes in my life, I told her, but if I said there was a god, never mind a God, well, that would be changing ... everything! And, it was way beyond where I was willing to go.

I wasn't sure if God existed, but if he did, I was sure he was a callous bastard. Why, if he had the ability to resolve all difficulty, were people starving in Africa or dying in car crashes? Never mind them —why was my life so balled up?

Rather than engaging in theological debate, the counselor just moved on to the next possibility, which was therapy. I went to my first therapist since the '60s for 10 visits, the maximum sanctioned by my health plan without approval from my primary care physician. When he declined to allow more, I angrily gave up.

Somehow, even though the first course hadn't helped, I didn't reject the process — it wasn't unpleasant, after all, for someone self-centered like me to sit around and talk about myself for an hour each week. After changing insurance plans to improve my therapy options, I went back for another referral. This encounter lasted nine months before I ended it, unconvinced it was having an effect.

Although a logical person would have to wonder why, I eventually went back for a third try. I can't imagine I would have tried a fourth time, but I never needed to find out, because that's when I was led to Bob Deutsch.

He was roughly my age or perhaps a bit older, moustachioed, bespectacled, and cardiganed. He was married with children and vastly more settled than I was; I'm fairly sure we would never have chosen each other to hang out with. But I found in him someone I could trust, a gentle guy without being a pushover, skilled at guiding our conversations without my realizing he was doing it. Most often, he would listen until I stumbled onto a point he considered important.

He once asked me, for example, if I'd had a good father when I was growing up. I answered that I couldn't know, because I'd only had one father, so I had no point of comparison. Some weeks later, I was expressing admiration for my brother's parenting skills, while wondering where he could have acquired them. Deutsch asked me what made Rich a good dad, and when I replied — constancy, availability, involvement, and whatever other qualities I cited — Deutsch swooped in for the score:

"Is that how your father was with you?" His point hit me like a barrel of bricks.

Um, no.

What makes Deutsch so impressive in retrospect is that he didn't need to fix me by himself. Other than my affiliation with him, the two monumental turning points of my coming transformation would occur outside his office, even though both resulted from his patient prodding. He not only helped me to see lots in my life that had been invisible to me, but he kept softening me up until I would accept the help I needed.

Meanwhile, my career was proceeding better than it should have, given my interpersonal issues. Maybe it was because my pluses were more easily quantified than my minuses. Or maybe it was just that journalism is notorious for spawning good editors but lousy leaders; I certainly wasn't the first social miscreant to advance in a newsroom.

My first promotion came a little more than two years after I joined the paper, and eight months later I was named senior editor of the weekend editions. The job is not unlike the job of managing editor (usually a paper's number two editor), in that it requires a broad view of all the paper's parts, rather than focusing only on sports, or metro, or features. And, most newspapers made half their revenues from the Sunday paper.

I reached that perch just before my 30th birthday, and someone ill-informed could have conjectured that I must be pretty impressive — I indulged in some of that thinking myself. But my rise was better explained by mere circumstance: I'd been assistant to that position when it opened, and no one else applied because it required working weekends. The hiring editors would have needed stronger reasons that I'd yet given them to reject me in favor of someone who hadn't wanted the job.

I would provide those reasons over two fitful, flailing years — a period during which I dropped any pretense toward dieting and packed on dozens of pounds, even while returning to regular exercise. When the demotion came, it was probably the smartest business decision Courant management had made regarding me since I'd been hired. Of course, that's not how I took it at the time. Even though my performance had brought me little respect, my work life was still the center of my esteem, and being reassigned was a deep humiliation.

It needn't have been. My new job was to repair a key part of the largest news expansion in the paper's two-centuries-plus history, and to all but the most involved observer, the move could have appeared as going from one high-importance role to another. One co-worker actually congratulated me. But I knew it was a demotion and insisted on correcting anyone who didn't. Certainly, it would have been better for me to allow, even encourage, the misconception, but quite literally, I could not help myself. Partly it was my revulsion for pretense, and partly it was the emotional payoff I got from proving what a truly sad case I was.

I've,ging that I attend support-group meetings, neither my eating nor my body size was changing much.

This is surely why, in the summer of 1991, Deutsch suggested that I again consider going to rehab. He hadn't made the prior suggestion; that had come a couple of years before I'd met him. In many ways, the work I'd done between those two points in time had been preparing me to change my response.

I didn't think I'd moved on the God issue, but it was no longer a deal-breaker. In fact, I didn't even raise the point when Deutsch made his suggestion; I just said OK, though it would be autumn before arrangements were complete.

These included approvals by both insurer and the Courant, and though I don't know what they were legally required to accommodate, I've always thought publisher Mike Waller, editor David Barrett, and news editor Marian Prokop went well beyond. Not only did they warmly encourage me to go, they agreed to hold my job and to pay my salary while I was gone. Because a colleague was going through a divorce and needed a short-term place to stay, I even got rent for my apartment.

My health insurer, meanwhile, agreed to pay 80 percent of the cost of my treatment, which I recall as standard coverage for the time, and the hospital, quite readily, agreed to waive the other 20 percent.

My diagnosis was, to me, questionable. If you'd asked me why I was going, I would have said it was because I was fat. Under interrogation, I might have gone so far as to concede that maybe I wasn't very well-adjusted either. But neither of those reasons would have satisfied an insurance carrier.

No, to get the dough, I'd have to be diagnosed with an approved affliction, and someone came up with obsessive-compulsive disorder. It wasn't that outrageous — I did obsess about food, and I did eat compulsively — but no doctor had ever suggested I had that disorder until someone wanted someone else to shell out 50 grand with me as the reason. If I'd been paying closer attention, I might have questioned the ethics of the situation, but I just wanted the green light.

On the appointed morning, my brother accompanied me on the three-hour drive south to Amityville, Long Island, where I would do nothing less than begin the rest of my life.

4

Getting What I Came For

IF I'M SO SMART how did I end up in a mental hospital?"

In the years since 1991, I've fallen back on that line often as I've shared the story of how I crawled out of misery, isolation, and cluelessness and joined the stream of human life. Going into rehab for food addiction wasn't the only step, but it was a key juncture, in part because I finally started to understand that my thinking wasn't as valuable as I thought it was.

Before I went in, most people would have said I was a very smart guy. But they'd also have said I was arrogant, childish, capricious, inconsistent, self-centered in the extreme, and as big as a house. So no matter how smart I was, I sure didn't have life figured out.

That's one of the facts of my life that I learned in rehab.

South Oaks Hospital sprawled over 90 acres of grass and grand oaks that were crisscrossed with roads and paths leading to meeting halls, classrooms, and residences. In them, in addition to the eating disorders unit, were wards for drink, drugs, gambling, sex, adolescent and geriatric psych, and many more.

The Eating Disorder Unit population fluctuated between 18 and 35 during my time, with the men never numbering more than 5. About half the patients were anorexics, most of them under age 20. Most of the problem eaters I've met in support groups outside of rehab have been overeaters, not bulimics or anorexics, but of course, bulimia and anorexia are official psychiatric diagnoses, so it was much easier for them to get treatment.

When I entered the unit, I thought I was ready for the experience, and in one principal way I was: I was determined to get what I'd come for. I didn't know what "it" would look like, but I knew that I had an unusual opportunity that wouldn't likely come my way again.

That's not to say I had surrendered; even if I might want only to be present, to do only what I was guided to do, I was unwilling (or unable) to stop interpreting and evaluating every direction, every suggestion, every nuance. All my strategies, all my defenses — all the habits I needed to change — were activated from the moment I signed in.

I would rather be able to report differently, that I was open from Moment 1. But if I hadn't had so many strategies and defenses that engaged whether I wanted them to or not, maybe I wouldn't have even needed rehab.

On my very first night, the evening session addressed self-esteem, and at the end, as an exercise, each one of us was required to identify a favorable part of ourselves. At first I was going to say that I care, but someone said that. Then I was going to say that I was funny, but two people said that. So I settled on "clever," which was eminently fair in my estimation.

The declarations by others had been quietly accepted by the group, so I was shaken and puzzled when mine provoked a buzz around the circle punctuated by comments such as "oh boy" and "we'll fix that."

Was it because I was new, or seemed arrogant, or both? I still don't know.

Meanwhile, I notice now, as I write, that I was unwilling to repeat what had already been said. That was allowed, and others had done it, but my automatic response was to set myself apart, and by cleverness to boot. What I needed more than anything was to join society, but my reflex was to do the opposite.

Clearly there was work to do, and I was in a place where I could do it. But I didn't yet even know the terms of battle.

My experience grew stranger on the second day, when they brought lunch to us on the ward, instead of trooping us to the cafeteria. The occasion was the weekly Feelings Meal, which was intended to connect food and eating to feelings.

I concede entirely that my overeating relates directly to my feelings, most often to my desire not to feel at all. When I stuff myself, I feel the distension of my stomach, or my more labored breathing, or the sting inside my mouth caused by the salt of a few hundred potato chips. Emotionally, I feel the remorse of having done this to myself again, mixed with the lust for the next gorge. But while I'm feeling those things, I'm feeling less of my loneliness, longing, and sadness.

Whether Feelings Meal subtly altered that equation, I cannot say by my experience. But I did pick up a good trick or two.

Limited by space, we were divided into two rooms in which tables had been put together and covered with sheets, the institutional tablecloth. Almost everything was individually wrapped, not just utensils but even slices of bread. Before the meal could begin, each of us had to collect every tool and morsel we would need and then discard everything we wouldn't — not only peelings and wrappings but plastic knives and drained salad-dressing containers.

During the meal, we were expected to eat silently and slowly, chewing each bite until "liquefied" and putting down our fork until we swallowed. As we ate, classical music wafted quietly from a boom box as a counselor laid on the rhetoric.

When we were finished, we were to wrap our napkins around our plates to signify to the proctor, and to ourselves, that the meal had ended. Often in restaurants today, I cover my plate with my napkin when finished, especially if the portion was more than I needed and some remains; it is amazing how much it helps. I know there's food under there, but somehow it's not there when I'm no longer looking at it.

I have even been known to wrap my dining partner's plate if something on it is calling to me, though almost always, I inquire first if she's done eating.

The surprise of Day 3 came in "primary," the first group therapy session of each weekday, in which the roster of individuals changed only when someone completed treatment or someone new arrived. That lent continuity to the proceedings, which were led by two counselors, each of whom had primary responsibility for half the patients in the room.

The assignment this Wednesday morning was to do a "social atom," in which we used symbols to represent family and friends. It helped introduce us to each other — especially me, the newcomer — but it also helped introduce me to me.

I put myself in the middle of the atom, with friends in one hemisphere and family in another. Then I realized: I don't think of anyone in my family as a friend. Huh.

There was space around me on all sides. Hmm: I can't think of anyone who is close to me. It wasn't until I saw someone else's atom, in which her mother was actually inside her own symbol, which she did to show their enmeshment, that I realized there were other ways.

Several others had symbols very close to them on all sides, and a counselor wondered if that wasn't suffocating. The opposite of that could be seen as room to breathe, but I saw it only as loneliness.

Part of the assignment was to note which elements of our atoms abused one or more substances, and again, I saw what I'd never seen before. More than half the friends I listed used one or more — most often pot and booze, with some cocaine — and I came to see it was no accident. Just as I had started smoking cigarettes in junior high school, in part, to gain entrée to a group, one thing the drugs did for me was to connect me with others in ways I had otherwise been unable to do.

But even more illuminating was that I didn't put a symbol on myself, which seems so completely impossible, and yet, there it was. If only for marijuana, or cocaine, I should have marked myself down.

But what about the food? I was in the eating disorders unit of a residential rehabilitation hospital! Might that have been an indication that I had a problem? Hadn't I also been attending eating-focused support-group meetings for at least a year, in which one of the keys was fully acknowledging that I had a disease that would ruin my life before ending it prematurely?

Yes.

But no, I didn't note that I had a substance problem when specifically asked. In my constantly judging head, I thought of it as a mistake, but it was an implicit expression of denial that would need to change.

Meanwhile, the group noted how small my symbols were, compared to the scale of the paper and to what others had drawn. The proper response would have been to listen closely and learn what I could, but I wasn't nearly ready for so sane a reaction. I responded defensively: Our directions hadn't said that scale was important, except that all the symbols should be of one scale, whatever we chose. I had done it right, damn it!

That evening, I noted in my journal — what is now a 20-year practice that started that week, on the instruction of my primary counselor Vivian — that I had been trying for weeks to psych myself up to follow the program and go wherever the counselors wanted to take me. But in my first opportunity in my primary group, I was the contrarian still.

One reason Bob Deutsch had given when he suggested South Oaks to me was that it had a gym. But when I got to the hospital, I had to await permission before I could engage in all but the lightest physical activity. This was one reason, during my first week, that I'd taken to returning from the cafeteria to the ward via an outside route, even though it was only 20 steps farther.

Most times, I would be with one or more peers, but Friday morning, I walked alone. The late October morning was damp, chilled, and still except for a light fog that wafted across the four-lane Sunrise Highway, which was beyond a fence perhaps a hundred yards away. Then a truck — a semi-style hauler with elongated trailer bed and relatively low sides divided by three stiffening uprights — lumbered out of the mist. In each of the bays created by the uprights was a word, making the sentence, "GET RID OF IT."

That was it. No phone number, no address, no logo. Just those big block letters.

In the first instant I figured it was some company's slogan. In the second instant, I was amused by a second meaning I could take from it, that I should jettison all the misconceptions and sorrow and rage that I carried inside of me. And in the third, I wondered if it could even be a divine apparition sent only to me.

The hauler had been really haulin', so by the time I pivoted to see if it had really been there, all that was left was a whorl in the vapor and a receding rumble.

Especially in a Google-ized world but even then, I could have found out if a trucking company on Long Island has such a slogan, but I've never wanted to. Even if it was merely a truck headed to its next mundane assignment, for me it remains one of the most mystical, ethereal experiences I've ever had.

Saturday mornings were reserved for Feelings Workshop. They were held in a couple of locations on campus and were open to patients both present and former. On my first Saturday, I fell in behind people I didn't know and ended up in a classroom with about 25 others. We sat in wooden school chairs that were way too small and placed way too closely together for comfort. As the session unfolded, my discomfort grew for other reasons.

The facilitator began by asking each of us to identify ourselves and to say what costume we would choose if we were dressing for Halloween. I said "clown," because they put on a happy face to entertain others, regardless of what they're feeling inside.

Sally, another of the group, said "ghost," and when we'd all had a chance, the leader came back to her to ask why. She said she wanted to fade away, because she'd been feeling so much anger and hurt, in part because of the sexual abuse she'd endured when younger.

As the sharing progressed, a half-dozen young women – that's one in four of the assembled – spoke about their abuse. One had been raped and said she blamed herself for not fighting harder, wishing her perpetrator had had a gun or a knife that could have explained why she hadn't. Two others spoke about feeling like "dirty little girls" for what had happened to them. Another one said she'd had two abortions but had never told her family in five years of pursuing loveless sex that had been triggered by abuse.

I'd never witnessed anything so intense, or real. And that was before Marcus, the only other guy in the room, spoke up. He had experience with abuse, too, he said, but he'd been the perpetrator, with siblings. He said he could nevertheless relate with others who had spoken, because he had carried guilt and regret with him ever since.

Rarely had I felt so moved, or afraid, or conflicted. How could these people be in the same room? How could the abused not lash out at an abuser? How could Marcus dare to reveal such a thing in front of these women? How could an abuser seem courageous, not for his actions when growing up but for his honesty now? I couldn't wait to get out of the room, and I didn't speak to anyone for hours.

I experienced madness of a different sort the next night. My roommate Virgil and I were watching the World Series: Game 7, 9th inning, and neither Atlanta nor Minnesota had scored. It was unprecedented, one of the most dramatic endings to a World Series ever. Tension with every pitch.

Then the clock struck 11:30 p.m., and the night nurse told us to shut off the TV and get to bed.

"But ... the game! Can't we say just a couple more minutes?" I asked, trying to explain to her that it was an extraordinary moment in a once-a-year event.

"Lights out at 11:30. Sorry," she said, betraying no sorrow at all.

"Could I trade a few more minutes for a restriction [the penalty patients got for breaking a regulation]?" I asked. It seemed like a fair deal: I wouldn't get away with anything, and I'd get to see the game.

Not only did she not strike the bargain, she threatened me with "a ticket to the Flight Deck," the locked ward where they sent recalcitrant patients. I appealed to the night counselors, but they offered neither aid nor solace. Faced with a Thorazine nightcap, I slinked away in outrageous defeat, pissed off but good and convinced I had just met Nurse Ratched.

Because addiction is a family disease, effective treatment brings families into the process. That's why families were invited to participate on Wednesday evenings and on weekends. Most of the patients lived nearby and their families came often, but my closest relatives were four hours' drive away, and each successive family member was further than the last. So I expected to go through the treatment as I felt I'd gone through childhood, all but alone.

I would be proven wrong repeatedly.

Rich was phenomenally supportive. Though it's true that he'd never needed something so drastic as rehab, he had done plenty of personal exploration, and had encouraged me as I started into it, and then further when I entered South Oaks. Time after time, he gave more than I expected, asked, or could have imagined.

Knowing that I'd wanted to bring some of my plants to care for but been told I could only have flowers, he sent a flowering plant with words of love and encouragement. They shouldn't have let me keep it – soil in a planter is a hiding place for contraband, I later learned – but it slipped through their screen. He also sent a stereo clock radio that gave me access to another comfort, music.

Not only did he deliver me to South Oaks and collect me at the end, he made the six-hour round trip five other times as well — seven times in nine weeks. He and Beverly came on their own, and Rich also came when my parents did, primarily to support me but also to participate.

My father and his wife, Kim, came on my second Sunday there for a session of "family bridge," a group encounter of patients and family members. It is impressive not only that they came first, but that they came at all. I had asked him to, but within the context of a letter in which I'd said angrily that

I almost hadn't told him I was going, certain that I could be gone for several months without his noticing.

But the session was disappointing, more because of my reactions rather than their actions. I confronted my father with my view that he had neglected us — me — as children, and he conceded as much. He said he felt guilty, and that he did love me. "He said that twice, but they were just words to me," I wrote in my journal. "I felt nothing, even though I can't recall his ever saying it before."

It was little better with Rich, when I turned to him to express my thanks for all he had done for me recently. This is what I wrote afterward: "I struggled with the same words Dad had given me. First I stuttered, then I said, 'I feel I love you.' Someone called me on it and asked if I really did or if I thought I did. I responded that I did, but I can't say I really felt it."

Nine days after they visited, I received letters from both Dad and Rich to which I reacted vastly differently. I barely noted my father's, while my brother's propelled him even higher in my pantheon.

I wrote in my journal that Rich's was "an extraordinary letter that was part exhortive, part sympathetic, part apologetic, part informative," and more. He described corporal punishment that he received from our mother that I hadn't recalled; I inferred that, at a minimum, I'd witnessed such acts, and reluctantly concluded that I'd probably experienced them, too. He apologized for all the times he'd beaten me up, put me down, and held me back, and confirmed what I hadn't consciously realized, that he'd regarded me as a rival to his mantle as number one son.

I brandished the letter in primary the next morning, as if it had done nothing less than give me a right to be on the planet.

My father's letter, meanwhile, languished for days. I'd expected nothing from it — nothing private, certainly — and had asked a friend to read it aloud. It said things I should have liked to hear — "that his aloofness doesn't mean he doesn't care, and other niceties" was my journal commentary — but I'd all but written him off after he'd visited.

"Now he writes a letter — one of **very** few he's ever sent to me — with statements that go against what I thought I'd finally learned, that he's in-

capable of showing, or having, emotions. So it's confusing," I wrote, con-
cluding that there must be reasons for all but ignoring the letter, and that I
didn't know what they were.

It occurs to me today that I still haven't responded to it.

Though that was the end of Dad's involvement, Rich just kept showing up.
The next week, he and Bev drove down for a Wednesday night event — af-
ter he'd worked all day, they packed the kids into the car, dropped them at
Bev's parents' house, and completed the three-hour-plus trip.

Unlike when he'd come with Dad and Kim, I was excited and delighted to
see them; I don't know if it was because Dad had been a damper, or if it was
the letter, or if it was just evidence of general progress. Regardless, the hugs
felt real this time.

Many addicts, when they finally decide to get help, come only to stop doing their one problem — whether it's drinking, bingeing, or running coke
— and end up learning that there's a whole lot more involved than just one
substance or behavior. That definitely happened to me.

I had come to deal with my eating, but relatively early in my treatment, my
counselors made an issue of the marijuana I'd smoked since freshman year. I
was surprised, and my first reaction was to say that I'd address it, eventually,
on my schedule.

That schedule turned out to be much shorter than I'd expected, as reasons
to stop started piling up. The first ones were little: In a health and nutrition
lecture, for example, I learned that pot's active ingredient remained in fat
cells and retarded weight loss.

In some other session, someone brought up the "munchies," the well-
known urge to pig out after getting stoned. For a compulsive eater like me,
they were more a concept than an experience since I'd been pigging out
for decades, on pot or off. But because my smoking buddies would join in,
the munchies had made it less necessary to sneak my binges, and therefore
easier to engage in.

So I began to see how pot could threaten my food recovery, even if I wasn't ready to capitulate on conventional grounds, that marijuana was a drug, and that addicts like me shouldn't be doing drugs. I don't know if, by themselves, they would have been enough to make me stop, but the point was rendered moot the next Sunday, when my pen lanced my marijuana habit forever.

I was in New York City, waiting for a friend to share my eight-hour pass, when I undertook an assignment from the EDU staff to write about my life as a pothead. I was angry to have to do it, but certain enough it was a fool's errand that I embarked upon cavalierly, unafraid of what might reveal itself on the page.

I wrote, arrogantly, that I knew I was the master of my pot use because, for example, I never went to work stoned. Work was important to me, and I'd always been able to put it first. That's when Yogi Berra's fat lady began to sing, right there under the vast, ornate ceiling of Grand Central Station.

I was stunned instantly by the implication, that life outside of work **wasn't** important to me. Dozens of times I'd gone to sleep with errands planned for the next day, only to start bonging upon awakening and still be on the couch at sundown, the day frittered away.

In the days ahead, I noted the sadness and anger of spontaneous mourning over the change, even as I feared the consequences for all my relationships that had pot in their foundations. But the issue had been settled. Only once have I smoked any pot since, when a college pal pulled out a bone in a parking lot before we went to a Patriots/Chargers game in San Diego.

Fifteen years' behavior, ended in a couple of paragraphs. I still marvel over it.

But the significance was even greater than that: I'd been willing to admit, at least to myself, that I'd been wrong — about the pot, certainly, but more than that, for being so defiant when Flo, the other counselor in my primary group, had given the assignment. It had turned out to be really useful, but I hadn't wanted to admit that to her because it would mean having to backtrack on my certainty that it was a dumb idea.

I'd been especially averse to it because it had been Flo, against whom I'd already developed resentments for grievances real and manufactured, mostly petty but large in my world view. I had done the same many times before — fallen into conflict with someone of authority and had that become the principal issue of the relationship, rather than heed any guidance or instruction. It was never to my benefit, but somehow to my comfort.

Instead of addressing the issue, or just knuckling under, I would continue to fight, usually passive-aggressively, and I'd been doing that with Flo.

In one case within primary group, she'd insisted that everyone give feedback to a peer, and she seemed very much the prosecutor who knew the answers to her questions; she was going to prove her point through our words.

I wouldn't have lied to the peer just to foil Flo, but I was evilly gleeful, inwardly, when I realized that giving a truthful answer would upset her plan. Had I not been in conflict with her, I still would have said my truth but I could have easily said something to the effect of, "while my experience wasn't that way, I can see her point, because..." Instead, I blew her out of the water.

In the outside world, hard feelings on both sides would have hardened further, and probably would never have been addressed. But because this wasn't the outside world, I got an opportunity to get beyond the conflict when Flo came to me after the session to talk about "our power struggle," and even a second one a couple of hours later, after I realized with the help of a peer that I'd left too much unsaid.

I can't say that either was particularly rewarding; we didn't part as friends, certainly. But it was significant in several ways: First, I felt acknowledged just by the action of her reaching out, even if I didn't find her answers very helpful.

Second, even if, in this case, she did the reaching, I saw the value of reaching out to someone with whom I was experiencing conflict; I've done it many times in the years since, and almost always with positive result. I expect that without rehab and support groups, I would have gone on, forever deepening conflicts until they were unresolvable, and then just cutting off contact.

And third, I did get one piece of really practical feedback during the second conversation: Flo said she was certain that I wasn't reacting to her, personally, but to traits I had experienced — and developed an aversion to — elsewhere in my life.

At the time, I wrote in my journal that "the notion had merit, but so far, I can't place it." Let's see: A strong-willed woman in a position of authority whom I experienced as overbearing, even manipulative. Nope, I couldn't think of anyone.

In person, my mother participated in my treatment twice, but figuratively, I brought her with me through the admissions office door and she rarely left my side. Where my childhood complaint with Dad was lack of involvement, my mother was the opposite: She'd been my indomitable force, as much hector as supporter, always expecting more, no matter what.

Her first actual visit was uneventful, a family session the night before Thanksgiving. The plan was that she'd fly into Long Island for the Wednesday night family session, drive me up to Connecticut the next morning to spend the holiday at Rich and Bev's (I had a 14-hour pass), and then return on the weekend.

The visit to Connecticut was great. I felt welcomed by all, but especially my nieces Sarah and Alex, who were too young to fake their delight when I arrived. And the food proved no particular temptation, particularly the nut-and-grain-filled gourd that stood in for the traditional bird, complete with construction-paper ears and beak, in their vegetarian household. Except the "turkey," the gathering was like most family holiday gatherings.

Around 6, my mother started pushing for Rich and I to get on the road so that I wouldn't return late. As I pointed out to her, we had made the trip in under three hours that morning, and I still had four-and-a-half hours before I had to be back. It was true that we planned to stop at my apartment in Hartford, but still, there was plenty of time, and besides, I told her, they weren't going to throw me in chains if I didn't arrive on the dot.

The truth was, I didn't want to engage with her on the facts. In recent years, as I'd begun to grow self-aware, I'd made the point to her numerous times that I was an adult and could steward my own life. I'd tried to be diplomatic, allowing that because she was my mother, I'd listen to her viewpoint, but then I needed her to back off.

When she said it again at 6:05, and again again at 6:10, I confronted her yet another time: Rich and I were adults, I told her, and fully capable of making this decision. I tried to make it clear that I was experiencing this as intrusiveness, precisely the sort of behavior that had driven me to eat in the past.

Her response? "Fine, but you better get going."

Thanks, Mom.

The ride back with Rich, which was extended by heavy holiday traffic, was as extraordinary as the ride with Mom had been uneventful. I felt ready to reveal some of my darker secrets, including that I'd stolen money from the family growing up. I shared a couple of sexual embarrassments, and for the first time, we compared notes on our facts-of-life lectures from Dad, which I'd remembered most for the shame I'd felt and still held.

Rich asked if he could share my secrets with Bev, and I not only said yes, I was able to share with him my respect and affection not only for her, but for him for having chosen so well. Rich told me some secrets of his, too, particularly about the early part of his relationship with Bev.

When we arrived I told him that for perhaps the first time ever, I felt as though I really had a brother in the world.

(Note to Mom: You were right; we were late, about 30 minutes. And I was right; there were no consequences. Told ya!)

 On Saturday, Mom and Rich returned for another family bridge, which was uneventful, but afterward, the three of us continued talking. After touching on a couple of other family matters, Rich gave me a shove to share with Mom the secrets I'd told him in the car. I disliked it, but needed it.

I told her how I'd often shied from reporting bad news for fear of her reaction. For example, I'd often had nose bleeds when I was a kid, and after the first few, I'd taken to going into the basement and hoping they would stop by themselves, rather than seeking her help. Then we got to the stealing, from her envelopes and from Richdale.

I expressed sorrow and shame for my actions and for the anguish I knew I'd caused her. The only reaction she showed was to look at the ground and shake her head slowly. I don't know what I could have expected: I'd known about these events for 15-20 years; she was getting them dumped on her all in one pile.

I asked her what I could do to repay what I had taken — which is part of the spiritual program that I follow, to acknowledge my mistakes and to make restitution where possible — and she was very conciliatory; I ended up paying for her flight to Amityville, and that was it. Monetarily, it was well short of what I'd taken from her, but she said it was all she wanted. I've always thought she agreed to accept even that as part of my process, rather than wanting or needing recompense.

One of the benefits of being in a rehab community is that everyone's inner self is free to roam, and people act just like they do out in the world. For me, that meant I acted angrily as often as not.

Under Flo's questioning after an encounter in primary, for example, I saw that when I'd been ignored at home, I'd gotten angry but not expressed it, and that unexpressed anger had eventually became my strongest food trigger. The twist is that only a trained observer would have guessed that, because I expressed anger aplenty.

At South Oaks merely a week, I was introduced to their concept of "forced fun" and boy did it piss me off. I'd seen it on the day schedule and thought it'd be a chance for a board game, but their idea was for me to make leaves out of construction paper to decorate the ward for Halloween.

"I was totally prepared to have fun, the usual purpose of the period, but I didn't consider this to be fun," I fumed to my journal afterward. "Infantile, needless, useless, but not fun. I want to play Scrabble, but they wanted me to have fun by doing something less fun."

Of course, I felt the need to share my disapproval, and when it wasn't instantly recognized as correct, to continue sharing it through grumbling, sneering, and other tiny tantrums.

The next week, though, I went along with their forced fun and stumbled upon what could be called my family coat of arms. The order of the hour was to use crayons, and I decided to illustrate a little wordplay I'd come upon since arriving: In stabs of red, yellow, and orange, I wrote my last name, but scrunched the first and last letters to let the others stand out.

Rage was buried in my very name.

It's just coincidence, a parlor trick. Prager is the German word for someone from Prague, and so far as we know, we don't even have Czech ancestry. But it expresses a truth — about my past, my present, and potentially forever.

When I shared my work of art, Flo's feedback included her pronouncement that my anger was such a part of me that I shouldn't expect ever to be rid of it. Not great news, but she suggested I try to counter it by finding a gentler message in my name to draw, so that at least the ugly one wouldn't stand alone. It took me years, but now if I use mnemonic shorthand for someone trying to remember my last name, I tell them it's "prayer," except a "g" instead of a "y."

From rage to prayer — I couldn't have a better metaphor for my journey.

While at South Oaks, I got to know my anger almost as a separate entity — I saw how people acted when it wasn't around, how they reacted when it was, and how I reacted when they reacted. I got to see what happened when my anger was red-hot, and the way I often reacted when it cooled to blue.

An important lesson I saw was that I often moped around even when succor presented itself. It was as if, upon rescue, I wanted to stay imprisoned; attention was attention, even if it derived from being the hopeless loser. It was my corollary to the public relations maxim that there is no such thing as bad publicity.

Another form I took, in anger, was the silent seether: Suitably provoked, I would sit there, radiating such pain that I thought surely someone would come and rescue me. But in feedback I learned that while I thought I was shouting "come hither and help," what everyone was hearing was, "stay the fuck away from me if you value your life." What monumental self-sabotage!

I learned that more than any other emotion, anger was my stand-in for sadness. I could grumble, I could spew, I could menace, but to cry was simply unreachable, even when I was alone. So when, on my 44th day in rehab, I cried in front of everyone, it was real evidence of letting go.

I had spent the second half of that morning in biofeedback, a one-on-one therapy in the basement that I'd been sent to twice before. It wasn't widely deployed among my peers, and I have concluded that I was sent so often because they were trying to connect me with my feelings.

I found the practitioner, Gail, to be sympathetic and I'd regarded her office as someplace where I could vent about all the mean, horrible things that were happening upstairs. On this visit, however, she quoted results from a thorough psychological testing I'd undergone weeks before that said I had "overwhelming amounts of rage." She said that she'd been talking to the unit's director that morning, to the effect that the staff thought I'd been talking a lot but not feeling.

By the end of the session, which lasted twice as long as usual and caused me to be 30 minutes late for lunch, I was very disheartened, a feeling cemented by one of her last comments, "What if it doesn't get any better than this?"

Though I wonder sometimes whether it was all scripted by really clever psychological counselors, it probably was just coincidence that this took place on a Tuesday, so that my first activity upon returning upstairs was Feelings Meal. I felt like not eating at all — which should have been proof that a different emotion was afoot — especially when I had to scrounge through the remainders of everyone else's preparation to get set, and then found a hair in my salad.

An added coincidence was that it was my primary counselor Vivien's turn to narrate. Her parable was about a child who became lost in the forest but was able to survive on skills her parents had taught her, even when she felt like quitting. As she spoke, my agitation and fear dissolved into sorrow and I began to cry. I thought tears were merely welling up in my eyes, but soon became aware they were running down my face and staining my shirt.

During sharing afterward, I expressed my fear that I wouldn't survive the forest, that I would just lie down in the snow and die, that I would leave the hospital without getting "it." Vivien later commented that when I'd looked down at the tear stains, I seemed to think I was bleeding, as if letting people see me cry was the same as letting them see me die.

What was probably more true is that they were seeing me come alive.

Being in a sea of addicts was one of the features of treatment at South Oaks, and patients who were considered to be cross-addicted, or bordering on it, were routinely sent to other wards to attend their 12-Step meetings.

My first visit outside the eating disorders unit wasn't to the drug users' house across the way, but to the gamblers' ward in another part of the campus, reached by dirt road through woods. Hospital policy prevented giving patients rides, so as I walked through the darkened glen, I was trailed by a security guard driving at 3 m.p.h., his headlamps lighting my way. It struck me as odd, but that was nothing compared with what came next.

I had gambled in one form or another since junior high school, when I tried to book bets on the first Ali-Frazier fight. I say "tried" because I didn't understand that it meant more than just writing down other people's wagers.

I started playing poker for money in junior high, and by high school the stakes had become much higher than any of us should have been playing. I never got burned in any of the $500 pots that occasionally resulted, but I still lost enough that I needed to steal from the register at Richdale.

I began betting on football, too, though I didn't really indulge in it until my mid-20s, when I spent hours a week for two straight seasons, massaging a system I'd developed to analyze statistics. (It worked, too, or seemed to; I won 65 percent of my bets during that time, according to the stats I eagerly, endlessly tabulated.)

I started in on casinos in college. Junior year, I grandiosely persuaded the friend of a friend to drive the three of us from Athens to Atlantic City so

I could go to Resorts International, at that time the city's only casino. I, the big spender, would pay for everything. We drove 14 hours through the night, arrived at 11:30 on Wednesday morning, and I was tapped out by 1:30 on Wednesday afternoon. It would have been sooner, but the lines were so thick that it took a while to squeeze into a seat

I'd subsequently been to casinos in Las Vegas, Reno, northwestern France, the Czech Republic, the Bahamas, and on cruise ships to and from the Bahamas. I'd dabbled in the lottery, bingo, backgammon, and gin rummy. I'd lost thousands more than I'd won.

But I'd never considered myself to have a gambling problem.

Still, when the counselor told me one day that I was going to a Gamblers Anonymous meeting that night, I didn't argue. I know I hadn't yet surrendered to the wisdom of others, so I can only conclude I was in a less argumentative mood.

The meeting started off in roughly the same way that all the 12-step meetings I'd been attending there did, with a prayer at the beginning and self-introductions by first name only. Until then, the meetings had been led by a patient who facilitated the format but professed no special expertise. But this one was led by two recovering gamblers from the outside who would not only conduct the meeting but would give advice.

Besides me, one other person was in the room, a patient on the gambling ward, and the outsiders focused entirely on him. For him, the hospital was not only a treatment site but a hideout — from the sort of gamblers who collected their debts in flesh if not in cash. He said he owed them "in the mid five figures."

While he was ensconced inside, his wife was at home, of course, and he related that she had no idea that dangerous men intent on collection might come calling upon her. He put it to the elders: Should he tell her of the potential danger?

It seemed an obvious call to me, and I was shocked when one of the advisers said he didn't think so. They might not come, he said, and why tell her if she might otherwise not learn of the dire circumstances?

I was silent through most of the meeting, but on this question they involved me, possibly because my body language was screaming already. "Of course you have to tell her!" I blurted, though I don't recall its affecting the conversation. I never saw any of them again, so I don't know what he decided. I still wonder sometimes what happened to him. And to his wife.

In memory, the incident retains an unreal quality, as if it was concocted to teach me the sin of wagers. Even though we had 90 minutes and only four participants, I don't recall having time to share — or even to explain why I was there. Under a format where there was free discussion, I could have learned whether I seemed on the edge of a gambling addiction, in the eyes of gamblers who'd been far enough through the ringer to know a comrade when they saw one. But we only talked about the gambler, his damsel, and the gunsels.

Even if it was fake (and of course, it wasn't), it worked: I swore off anything approaching a bet for more than a year — I even resigned as manager and participant of the rotisserie baseball league I'd founded. But in a fit of willfulness when the bars closed down one night, I took off with a friend for Foxwoods, the Indian casino that had opened less than an hour from Hartford while I was in rehab. Back at the craps table for the first time, my body literally shook — I was rattled but I still rolled. I liken the episode to a friend's experience learning to chew tobacco with his college baseball teammates: It makes you feel horribly uncomfortable, but you keep trying until you're past it.

I gamble again now — I've taken back everything but the football and the bingo — but that one meeting with that one guy and the two elders left me with a visceral respect for where gambling could take me. I'm aware that the knowledge, by itself, won't keep me from going there, but I hope it'll let me see the approaching danger sooner, if I start in that direction. I know that addicts switch addictions, and as I wrote in my journal that night, in capital letters, it could be gambling.

As it does throughout medicine and insurance, a constant battle of interests governed the length of patient stays at South Oaks: The insurance company wanted to stop paying as soon as possible, and the hospital wanted to keep the spigots open. On my way out the door, I got caught in a collision of those interests.

Most of my peers got weeks to prepare to leave: Either they'd come in with a four-weeks-and-out plan, or they'd been given a release date three weeks out so they could begin sewing up all the incisions of treatment. Although I'd gotten an inkling in a phone call with my boss the previous week, I learned on Dec. 18, a Thursday, that I'd be leaving on Saturday.

My onsite shrink, who had an ever-shifting slate of patients and doubled as the unit's medical director, explained that, in the run-up to my treatment months previous, he'd told my employers that I would be done in December. He said it was his typical tactic not to ask for all the time at once, in effect to string the chumps along. Meanwhile, he said, he was in the habit of tailoring his progress reports to the concerned parties. To the insurer, he said, he typically emphasized the negatives, to argue for further treatment. To the employer, he was more positive, explaining that to do otherwise might affect a patient's long-term job prospects.

But because he'd failed to adjust his first estimate, the two parties had developed an expectation, and when confronted, he'd chosen the rosier picture as the accurate one, and so I had to go. Quickly. The hospital felt so regretful, he said, that they'd donate a half day on Sunday to accommodate weekend sessions with family that had been planned.

At that last session, on my way to making some other point, I shared that I kept baking chocolate in my kitchen cupboard. I did this to make chocolate mousse, even though I'd given up refined sugar months earlier.

I liked making the dessert for the artistic experience, how the color changed from blonde to deep brown, and how just adding whipped egg whites changed the texture from ribbony to fluffy. Just as important, I liked to please — and show off to — people who could eat it. Several times, I boasted to the group, I had made the dish without so much as licking a smear of it off my finger. The confection didn't call to me at all.

"That's impressive," a counselor said, "but when you get home, throw the chocolate out."

"But you don't understand," I replied. "It's been there for months. Never once have I taken it off the shelf except to make mousse, and never once have I even thought of eating it straight."

"That's fine," she said, "but when you get home, throw it out."

"But you don't understand," I repeated. "It's not a problem."

But she persisted, so when I got home, even before I had doffed my coat, I went to the cupboard, chuckling wryly at the silliness of their nonunderstanding, and threw the package out.

The willingness to let others be in charge, whether I thought they were right or not: That's what I'd come for.

5

Better, But Not Well

BECAUSE OF ALL THAT I LEARNED and all the changes I experienced, I have come to think of the day I went into South Oaks as my rebirthday, as special to me as most people regard the day they came into the world.

Over the next several years, my life would head in beneficial directions I had neither expected nor even contemplated: Relationships, work performance, and personal productivity all began to improve; I was able to take on challenges and expand creatively; I grew willing to see the world in new ways and to take responsibility for my actions. I started getting laid.

And that doesn't even broach what most people would consider topic No. 1: I lost weight in a balanced, sane, and healthy manner and kept it off.

I donated or dumped practically every piece of my wardrobe, and went from cloaking myself in stained, cigarette-singed schmattas to donning ensembles distinguished not just by jackets and ties but by suspenders and other accessories. Before I was done losing, I actually began giving away some of the replacements, because they no longer fit either. I developed a semi-emotional relationship with my tailor.

Though family vacations had taken me to more of the world than most people see, I hadn't traveled much on my own. And when I had, I'd done it poorly, such as on a trip to Paris, when I'd spent my evenings closeted with junk food in my hotel room, trying to fathom French television instead of exploring the City of Lights.

But now, I began to travel in a new way. Four months out of rehab, I melded half a dozen work friends with my brother and two of his college pals into a paddling crew for a rollicking ride down the upper Hudson River. Ours was the only raft of the convoy to flip, but I'd wager that we also had the most fun.

That went so well that I started looking for other ways to be adventurous, though in the wild, I didn't make it much farther. Rich and I took a hang-gliding lesson, but while he got airborne, I discovered to my embarrassment that those kites are heavier than they look. I briefly contemplated skydiving, until Rich reported after his leap that he'd never go back up.

I did, however, embark on a terrestrial travel plan in which my goal would be to find myself one day in some foreign locale where I knew no one and where no one spoke English. In June, I took the first leg of that journey.

To San Francisco.

OK, it's not a foreign country, and, yeah, they speak English there, and, well, I did have a couple of acquaintances I could call if I felt lonely or overwhelmed. But as a 3,000-mile first step, it was a gentle test of adventurousness and I passed, taking in the sights without being controlled by fear — and without junk food. When I did call those acquaintances, it was not out of desperation but of bonhomie.

A month after I returned, I stumbled into a breach in my long, desperate battlefront with the opposite sex. I regularly went to Harry's Pizza on Sundays after attending a support group gathering down the street, and Cathy, a fellow attendee, amiably invited herself along. We might have come together once before with a couple of others, and we may have talked on the phone once or twice, one compulsive eater to another. But neither of those were unusual, and this was as casual as could be.

Cathy worked in insurance, had been married, and owned her home. She had a weight issue as I did – it was, of course, what brought us into contact — but it wasn't pronounced, and her craziness around food was in the ballpark with mine. She was bright and curious; her most common rejoinder was, "Isn't that interesting!"

We were talking about nothing in particular when the topic turned to men and women and sex. It wasn't uncommon for me to steer such conversations in that direction, hoping I might discover the secret passageway into casual sex. I gave her my usual plaint, that women had all the control over when sex happened; her answer was anything but usual: "Well, if that's the problem, I'd be happy to service you."

Years later, I would come to the conclusion that most people do, that casual sex is rarely fulfilling, but at that moment, I was exultant and ready to roll in the hay. All that willingness/surrender/spirituality stuff was fine, but this was the sort of change I could get excited about. Cathy and I were never in love, but we clicked as enthusiastic lovers who found grounds for conversation as well.

Merely half a year out of the hospital, I was living a life transformed. This time, really, the deep-seated problem of a lifetime had been resolved, right?

No, not even close, again. I would venture much further into the mainstream than I'd ever gone, and fare better than I ever had at the margins, but I would still stumble repeatedly, not only with food but with the basics of everyday living. The '90s would be my halfway house, several rungs up from hell but with more to climb before reaching the cool, placid surface.

I had made progress, both in maturity and reduced body size, and that allowed me to experience large swaths of life that had been off-limits to me, especially around women. My less dreadful outer self made it less obvious that I had issues, which let me begin to play out all the Oedipal neuroses that had been fermenting since birth.

I was also measuring my progress by things like clothing, adventure, and sex, rather than by advances in traits such as willingness, surrender, and humility, as endorsed by Bob Deutsch, counselors in rehab, and peers in support groups. The advice I'd heard from them was to own up to all the sordid, sneaky, and petty crap of my past; to right the situations where appropriate; to trust God; and to help others. I had done little of it since leaving South Oaks, but got more motivated when my food plan seemed to get harder to follow.

Before leaving Amityville, on counselors' strong suggestion, I'd called home to Connecticut and enlisted a mentor to help me negotiate my new way of living. I'd met Michael in the Sunday night group, and I thought it would give us a common language. He told me to call him several times a week, and I did.

Now the fact that I'd gotten a mentor, and that I was actually calling him, was evidence that I was trying out a new path. But plenty of evidence suggested that I thought I was still in charge. For example, he'd said from the first call that I should get to work on the stock-taking and the housecleaning, and would often ask if I'd begun. But it wasn't until food obsession began returning that I did.

Also, he said that I should write a bit every day until I was done, that I would be rewarded by consistency, in addition to the details I'd gather. Instead, I decided to spew everything out in one day. My thinking — that is, my fear — was that if I didn't finish the project the day I started, I might never return to it.

But one of the major points of this new way of life was that it was supposed to be just that — a new way of life. As long as I continued as captain, I wasn't very likely to find a new route.

I also note, somewhat ruefully, that fear was my principal motivation — fear that I might be slipping back into old ways, then fear that I'd never finish if I didn't do it all at once. Abandoning the cudgel was part of the point of this new way, but even in service to a healthy aim — the stock-taking — fear was still guiding my way.

So I wrote my inventory over 11 hours on July 4, which some novelist would paint as an impulse for independence, but the choice was much more mundane: I had the day off.

Soon afterward, I sat down with Michael to read it to him, which was the next phase — to say aloud, before us and before God, who I had been and what I had done. There is a lot more to the recovery process than just writing and reading a list, but before I got to the rest of it, I began to lose contact with Michael and slowly drifted to the side of the road, at least regarding the important work. I did keep attending support groups, continued writing in my journal, and took enough other actions to think that I was still "working it," and hey, I was keeping the weight off, right?

This is not to say my eating was uneventful. My thawing social life led me to eat out more often, for example, and even at home, I started bending my very clear boundaries in what appeared, at least case by case, to be reasonable adjustments.

For example, I was supposed to eat four times a day, in the amounts and from the categories that had been prescribed at South Oaks. But when I started noticing that I didn't need the fruit assigned to lunch to feel satisfied, I started "reassigning" that fruit to my evening snack. Then I did the same for dinner, and soon, I had an evening "snack" that looked like my binges used to.

There are two points to draw from this: One: I was still making the decisions. I had been given a food plan by the nutritional authorities at South Oaks, and just because I'd followed it for a while didn't mean I was qualified to adjust it. If I'd wanted to change something, I should have gone back to them, or found a new authority — anyone but me would have suited. And two: If I'd had regular contact with a mentor, she or he would certainly have questioned those changes immediately.

Some might say the adjustments were no big deal — calories in, calories out, and nothing more. But those are the people who don't get it: For me and m̶   ̶rs like me, calories are not the only issue, even if the math
        ̶ng my lights to guide what I ate had been ruinous for years.

        ̶ of this contention is in what comes after. To be absurd
        ̶e wants to eat all their calories for the day at high noon,
        ̶that, it's good for them, I guess. And if I had thrived on
        ̶at. But once I started to fiddle with an externally pro-

vided eating plan — especially when not fiddling had proved so successful — where would the fiddling stop?

My first "official" binge came on Aug. 25, 1993, just over 20 months after leaving South Oaks. Not by design but not surprising in retrospect, my journal entry began by noting the timing:

"I ate last night, utterly overboard, for the first time since leaving the hospital. Popcorn, more popcorn, an apple, a jar of peanuts, and a bagel, half of it with cream cheese. Started at 2:30. Didn't get to sleep until almost 7." (It's worth saying that, today, I don't eat popcorn, peanuts, bagels, or cream cheese. For me — and each food addict's list is different — they all are in the category an alcoholic puts alcohol: I have used up my life's supply, having proven that I cannot use them casually.)

For the skeptics, I'll concede that one harsh eating episode is evidence of nothing, in itself. But for the rest of the millennium, I would rarely go more than a month without some sort of boundary-busting food episode, some of which snowballed into severe, weeks-long binges. I never quit my support structure, but I strained to accommodate both spiritual growth and bacchanal.

At my worst, I grew to 260 again, though typically, I fluctuated within a not-awful 10- or 15-pound range near my lowest weight. I concede that's pretty impressive, when the worst is more than 100 pounds less than where I started, and unquestionably, I was delighted to be well removed from my formerly freakish proportions. But I wasn't really healthier; I was just less rotund.

I expect that some people who've struggled with their weight for years will consider me a greedy whiner, and think that if they could just get near their goal weight and keep it there, that'd be plenty. I can certainly relate: It's what I thought in high school, it's what I thought when I had my chest taken in; and it's what I'd been thinking in the first seasons after rehab.

But it **still** wasn't so. Sure I was thinner, but I was still trying to direct the world's outcomes, and still prone to slashing my own way through the wilderness instead of joining up with others who knew the way.

This isn't to say that I wasn't getting better. In the same way that I'd lost a lot, if not all, the excess weight I'd carried, I had made strides interpersonally, even if I still had work to do. At the Courant, I'd been personally and professionally rehabilitated, in part because the contrast to my former self was so marked. As pleasing as that was, I eventually decided that Hartford was not where I wanted to live the rest of my life.

Just a week after that "official" binge — the timing may not be coincidental — I got the offer I'd been courting since June, to work at The Boston Globe. Not only would the Globe be a big step up professionally, but it would be a particular plum for me, who'd delivered the paper as a child.

I valued my network of peers and support meetings in Hartford, and would be sad to move away from Rich, Bev, and the girls, but I knew I would find counseling and recovery programs in Boston too, and it was my hometown. My dad and his wife lived in town, and Mama Ruth, my mother's mother, was still living independently at 87 on the North Shore, about a half-hour away. We'd developed a close relationship the last time I'd lived in Greater Boston, about 9 years earlier.

My first act upon moving — before I reported for work, before I looked for an apartment — was to seek out a meeting. It was partly a symbolic act, to put the continuation of my emotional and spiritual recovery first on my docket, but it was also a concrete practicality: I needed to establish that part of my life immediately.

My experience that day turned out to be symbolic of something else, however: My move would not be nearly as seamless as I would want. At the meeting's beginning and ending times, I was the only one there, though three people attended for portions in between. What I heard was more stern, almost militaristic, than what I'd known in Hartford, and I feared I wouldn't thrive in that sort of atmosphere.

My entry into a new workplace was fitful, too. Though I'd been eager for the chance to enter a setting in which I was neither the fat guy nor the guy who'd lost a lot of weight, I still found, semi-involuntarily, plenty of ways to set myself apart.

Partly, it had to do with food: While most everyone would bring a sandwich or go to the cafeteria, I'd bring fully cooked, well apportioned meals, and before long, I'd be explaining why. In spite of myself, I became the guy who talked about how much weight he'd lost.

Another way in which I stood apart, I didn't actually stand apart at all. I found the atmosphere on the night copy desk to be harshly negative, out of proportion even to the standard cynicism required of journalists in general and copy editors especially.

A couple of my colleagues would routinely and loudly roast any work by our newest foreign correspondent, without a whit of compassion for how hard it was to establish oneself in a foreign land, in a foreign language, living alone. And a desk supervisor would regularly sing "don't want to be here, don't want to be here, don't want to be here no more," to a tune no catchier than the lyrics.

In Hartford, I had undertaken to remove the rampant negativity that rehab had revealed in my thinking. But in Boston, once the bloom was off my new workplace, my negative waves started rippling again. My "justification" was all the negative people around me, as if my brand of negativity was somehow better. In fact, it was worse: As a garden-variety grouser, I'd at least have been part of the gang. I was as bad as them while acting as if I was better.

Then, just weeks after I started, the editor who'd championed my hiring moved to a different position and I came under someone both less benevolent and less impressed with my skills. I did indeed become garden-variety — yet another worker not sufficiently valued by the boss — though still without fitting in.

Meanwhile, my move homeward opened vast new territory in my long-running quest for a girlfriend. In Hartford, I hadn't gone much beyond gleeful rutting, but after less than two weeks in Boston, I embarked on my first-ever serious significant-other relationship.

In Roxanne, one of the newspaper's powerhouse editors, I found someone who was primed to settle down. She was a bit older than me, had been in a decade-long relationship that hadn't ended well, and, I think, was going to marry the next acceptable candidate.

Unfortunately for her, she was open to my interest. What she saw was a spiffy-dressing, well-spoken man in his mid-30s, and I was those things. But like most addicts, my age emotionally was substantially younger. Clinical wisdom holds that when an addict picks up his or her substance, emotional maturing stops, by which measure I was 12 or so.

We lasted seven months, which in my world was a very long time, though she would probably describe it as a brief and wasteful interlude. So far as I know, she did marry her next serious partner — I got to read more details about it than I wanted from a column she wrote for the Globe magazine.

I got a lot from the relationship, but above all else, I learned what it was like to be the partner who wanted less than the other one did. Over the next several years, I would take on the other role repeatedly, chasing after women who didn't want to be caught — at least not by me. Every time, my reaction was a binge. Clearly, this wasn't celebration, but it wasn't consolation either; it was punishment, for aggressively pursuing failure, yet again.

I didn't binge only over women, though it was by far the "best" reason I had. But other times, I didn't have — or couldn't identify — a reason. I was, and remain, in the habit of cooking when I had the time and then assembling cooked ingredients at mealtimes. When I'm in healthy spiritual condition, that works just fine; no dish, not even the most inviting ones, is the enemy by itself.

But if my spirit is weak — and it's not like you can just pull the dipstick to check — anything can happen. More than once, for instance, I'd roast a chicken for the next few meals, and then decide to pinch off "just one little corner" of particularly appetizing skin, and before I could stop, I'd have eaten all of it, and sometimes even started in on the soft bones and cartilage, dipped in salt. (Sorry; yes it's gross, but also further proof of food insanity.)

I could lurch from binge to binge because they were spread just far enough apart to classify them as slips, rather than relapse. But if a rejection came while I was already unstable with food, I would go from patches of trouble to nightly $15 expenditures at the nearest 7-Eleven.

In April 1996, one of these "slips" had stretched into a fifth month and people started asking me when I was going back into rehab. Faced with that unpalatable prospect, I instead acceded to my therapist's persistent urging to try antidepressants. Theretofore I had been adamant: "Sure I'm off my game sometimes, but I can handle it, damn it, so leave me alone."

It wasn't until much later that I realized that I'd held that attitude for a very long time — about food! "Sure, I eat too much sometimes, but I can handle it, damn it, so leave me alone."

It turns out, I had quite a few ties between overeating and depression:

Like most people, I viewed both as moral instead of medical issues. "I **should** be able to do better, and I **can** do better — I just have to try a little harder."

In both instances, my failures to cope reinforced the maladies I was trying to overcome, whether chemically or emotionally: Overeating begat more overeating, and the grimy gauze of depression helped confirm that I really was a worthless slug.

The experiences came years apart, but in both cases, I submitted to strong action only when the pain sustained itself long enough that I cried uncle. In the case of antidepressants, I didn't become willing until it was framed as the option easier than returning to rehab.

Food and depression often chase each other: food abuse can trigger a depressive episode, and a depressive episode is a trigger to eat. I don't argue that these are exclusive — I haven't eaten unbridled for at least five years, and I have definitely been depressed during that time. But I am certain that abusive overeating — particularly using refined foods such as flour and refined sugar — made some of my episodes worse.

It's not radical, of course, to suggest that people rely on substances to distract from psychic pain. Nor is it radical to suggest that some people who begin that sort of behavior out of choice — with alcohol, or cocaine, or sex, or shopping — eventually run out of options and begin doing it habitually. And it shouldn't be radical to suggest that the same thing happens with a pint of Ben & Jerry's, or a loaf of cinnamon raisin toast.

After six months of psychopharmacological fine-tuning, the savagery of my eating receded, and I went back to just occasional trouble for several months.

It's worth pointing out that I was also working concurrently with a recovery mentor during this time, and that he had been dogging me to take stock again, just as I had done after South Oaks. In early August, I reported that I still hadn't finished, and he replied, "Well then, you get to keep on binge-ing," and I did.

Because of the antidepressants, or not, I did finally complete the exercise, took the further actions of asking God to remove the troublesome portions of my personality that had been uncovered, and began making restitution where called for. One of these was West Lynn Creamery, which had oper-ated the Richdale store I'd stolen from as an employee during high school. I didn't know how much I owed, but settled on $1,000 in cash as recom-pense.

I have felt a bounce from taking that action, and do feel freer when I drive by their headquarters on my way to the North Shore, but my absurdly in-ordinate mooning over a failed relationship kept pulling me back into an eddy of food abuse, so that within a year of beginning the antidepressants, I'd written in my journal that I'd "concluded that rehab is the right move. Now I have to arrange it." But then I rebounded enough, again, and my resolve dissolved into six more months of eating.

I finally did go away in the beginning of October, to a long-weekend work-shop at The Willough rehab facility in Florida, but it stopped the bingeing only for a few weeks before I started slipping again. I had another round about six months later, bingeing the night before I was supposed to leave for the Jazz Fest in New Orleans; I missed my flight and burned a swath through the terminal's food court before limping back home in shame. A month later, I paid $800 to fly to Ottawa, in addition to the tuition for another Willough event, this one for Canadian alumni.

Though I did significant work that weekend, I didn't even make it home before I'd picked up illicit substances again. My flight was canceled, so I had to get a motel overnight and make do for dinner at a mini-mart next door. I chose popcorn and pork rinds, and the measure of value for my weekend was that I chose to stop eating before I'd emptied either (big) bag.

After a couple of swift hook-ups with women in August and September kept the slide rolling, I wrote in my journal, "Food and women. Remove those two subjects and there's practically nothing left in this journal." At Christmas, I weighed in at the gym at 240.

Within a year, two new threads of discontent would send me back for more rehabilitation on a scale I hadn't seen since South Oaks.

The first began when I agreed to lead the Globe's features copy desk. It was clearly a soul-crushing job and I didn't want it, but thought if I could survive, I'd be rewarded with a job that I would want. I would never get to test my calculus, though, because it chewed me up and spewed me back out before very long at all.

It can't be coincidental that most of the key players were women who would not go along with what I had in mind. Mostly, I'm referring to the shrewish crew of bitter copy editors whom I utterly failed to lead effectively. Some were openly rebellious, while others would smile to my face and then send poison-cursor e-mails to each other about me. This isn't (only) paranoia — on two occasions I accidentally received mail that was about me, not intended for me.

Playing opposite my recalcitrant wards was an oft-spineless boss who would endorse initiatives I proposed, only to back off at the slightest pushback from below. I'll never forget when I told her that one of them, Sally, would not like my plan, and was sure to complain. The boss said, "Don't worry, I'll deal with that." So I told Sally the plan, Sally marched in to the boss, and the boss summoned me: "Do we have to do this?"

That's management by a pro, ladies and gentlemen. (I can scoff all I want. My way of doing things left my career damaged and my life in shambles. She rose to be the No. 3 editor at the paper.)

The second looming thread was a bit later in developing, and had a far greater upside; her name was Ida. Although eventually, events in our relationship would help send me to my lowest bottom, we lasted more than a year together, had many happy moments, and even talked marriage.

Both these tendrils were growing in the first quarter of 1999. The crash at work came in March, when I demanded out of my post at whatever career cost. I could hardly have gone less gracefully, telling my colleagues what I thought of them on my way back to my old chair, right next to theirs.

Though I had very little serenity or safety around food, my weight was actually declining, because I was controlling it in yet another questionable flanking tactic: I began drinking to oceanic excess, "just" diet sodas and decaf coffee. Sure, this was better than, say, milkshakes, but it was still just a method for staying full. And then I decided to go for the milkshakes anyway, sort of: I devised a mixture of instant decaf coffee, powdered low-fat milk, several packages of Equal, and ice in a blender, so that I could enjoy a "free" and frothy treat.

Free? Well, I drank decaf already, so that was OK. Sometimes I'd put milk in it, so that was no big deal either. And I'd been going through those little blue packets like water, so what was a few more? And what could be more innocuous than ice — it's just frozen water, right? Free!

Except no. Not even close.

Even to a devious chipper like me, this should have been beyond acceptability, but I clearly favored denial over being denied. Let me count the ways that this was insanity in a large plastic cup:

One: I went from having none of these to having two or three a day. Never mind the substance; the behavior alone should have been reason for concern.

Two: When I wasn't having one, I was thinking about having one.

Three: Calorically, the powdered milk was well beyond any milk I'd been having in my coffee. And the milk in my coffee wasn't on my food plan.

Four: The farting! The concoctions brought such havoc to my digestive tract that I couldn't help but herald my dirty little secret to all who came within nose- or earshot. This wasn't even the first time I'd courted ostracism for a fix; sugar-free candy has the same effect, especially when you eat it a pound at a time.

How far would I not go to feign abstinence while still getting hits off food?

When the Jazz Fest came around again at the end of April, I actually boarded the plane this time, and I wrote in my journal, upon returning, that food had been "OK." But I also mentioned that for the purpose of my food plan, I'd equated fruit with pork cracklin's fried fresh at the fairgrounds. I'd spent $9 on orders of them, an amount that surely would have been higher had they not run out well before I was done eating them. (I'm fairly sure they would have run out anyway.)

Though I held on to my ragged recovery with white knuckles for a couple more months, I began my last (well, most recent) great slide to a bottom a couple months later, when I headed down to Baltimore to take in a weekend of baseball at Camden Yards with friends.

The first debauch was Saturday night at a crab house. The overeating itself was not proof of doom, for many times I'd eaten untowardly in a restaurant and then just resumed my plan the next morning. But being out of town was another danger point: I'd always been more likely to skid on the road.

The clincher arose the next day. My plan was to head to D.C. for a couple of days of museums, and after the game, I caught a ride south with a friend returning to Virginia. I love this guy, but what I remember is that I couldn't wait for him to let me off so I could eat whatever I wanted.

Once we parted, I made a half-hearted attempt to find a grocery store where I might get appropriate food before settling in for a few hours in a coffeehouse, where I swilled iced espresso until closing, and then rationalized an evening snack of an apple and a bag of high-end potato chips. Even that could have been OK, if I'd been stable emotionally. But I was not.

When I got to my hotel, I denuded the minibar of every morsel I could justify, and then headed back into D.C.'s mean streets after midnight, determined to find a place with junk to peddle. And, of course, I didn't come back until I had.

A week later on the Fourth of July, back at home, I wrote in my journal, "My fingernails are shot, as short as they can be without bleeding. And, fluids, fluids, fluids! Maybe the binge last weekend shouldn't have been such a surprise. It's just different substances. I sure didn't savor the stuff I ate. I stuffed it in, just like the fluids."

Later that day, Ida and I watched Boston's famed fireworks in a crowd dominated by children, triggering a discussion on having kids. We had been getting along well enough that it was an appropriate topic, but she wanted them and I didn't. In retrospect, I'd say our relationship hit its height just before that conversation started.

At the end of the week, I traveled again, back to Ohio to meet up with about 30 friends for an unofficial college reunion that I'd looked upon as a victory lap, in which I could "show them all" how non-fat, and non-loser, I'd turned out. I probably pulled off the showing, but I overate at a couple of the joint meals. On Sunday morning, I spent time with my two closest friends from college and all went wonderfully well. We pledged to stay better in touch, and I returned home in high spirits and at high rev.

Two days later, Ida told me she was taking a job in Vermont.

I'd known she was going for an interview; hell, I'd encouraged her to go when she wasn't disposed to, on the grounds that the interview would be good experience. But I had no clue that she'd get an offer, or that she'd take it, or that she'd take it before we got to discuss it.

I know — and knew then, mostly — that she was taking an action for her life and career, and not one calculated to hurt me, and I did my best to be supportive. I even canceled a trip I'd planned, and paid for, to Amsterdam with my brother and his family because it would conflict with her moving date, and who was going to help her if I wasn't?

But emotionally, I was floored. I don't know if I would have survived such a blow on firm food footing, but in the muck where I was mired, it was the kill shot.

6

Itinerant Rehab

EIGHT YEARS EARLIER, I had retreated for 54 days to a fully staffed hospital on 90 landscaped and wooded acres on Long Island. The patient population of the eating disorders unit never went below 18 and tended to be around 30, and we were attended by about 20 psychiatrists, counselors, administrators, and nurses.

This time, I decamped for five days to a rented vacation home 40 minutes outside Louisville with about a dozen others — including the staff, Phil Werdell and Mary Foushi.

I would have been happy to return to Long Island, but for people like me, South Oaks was simply no longer there. The institution survives even today, but it had shuttered its eating disorders unit in 1998.

No one would argue that eating disorders had gone away, so what happened?

The general answer: Managed care tightened the parceling out of medical services nationwide, including for rehab.

The specific answer: Even in the context of managed care, insurers cracked down on services for problem eaters. You'll remember that at South Oaks, I didn't actually get treatment for obesity, even though I spent my time in the eating disorders unit. The Diagnostic and Statistical Manual of Mental Disorders, which issues diagnostic criteria from the American Psychiatric Association, simply didn't (and still doesn't) recognize my experience as a disease, so my stand-in diagnosis was obsessive-compulsive disorder. But even that sort of dodge came under attack just about the time I was entering South Oaks.

A Place For Us, a Florida company that had treatment relationships with hospitals in four states, was sued by 21 state Blue Cross Blue Shield plans alleging, among other charges, that patients had been recruited with promises of obesity treatment, but then had been diagnosed with depression, bulimia, or others illnesses that were billable to insurers.

The case made minor headlines for several years, in part because the suit, and a similar action by Aetna that followed, reportedly ran concurrent with a federal criminal investigation that never amounted to much.

Janet Greeson, the operator of A Place For Us who herself had lost 160 pounds and written the best-selling "It's Not What You're Eating, It's What's Eating You" before opening A Place For Us, never conceded wrongdoing. She pointed out that her centers could have enticed no one without physicians' diagnoses. She accused insurers of trying to avoid charges they had already sanctioned, and countersued. The parties eventually settled, but by then, Greeson's network was in shambles and she'd spent thousands in legal fees.

By 1999, the attack on A Place for Us had so devastated the field that I soon realized I couldn't hope for any insurance support, which ruled out traditional rehab. So I turned to Acorn Food Dependency Treatment Services, which I'd become aware of when Werdell helped lead a weekend retreat I'd attended the previous spring.

Phil had been a counselor at Glenbeigh Hospital in Tampa, which was not unlike South Oaks, from 1987 to 1993; when he left, he was asked to help shepherd the hospital's alumni-weekend program. He'd relocated to Seattle and opened a private practice for problem eaters, but the first year, he and a partner conducted more than two dozen weekend programs all across the country, wherever a pocket of Glenbeigh alumni justified the effort. The events were free to patients as an aftercare benefit.

Then the mother ship at the other end of the tether went under, not as a result of poor treatment outcomes but of untenable real estate investment financing. In bankruptcy's wake, Phil and two others decided to continue offering the service, with two important changes: Participants would have to pay, and participation would be open to anyone.

What resulted was essentially a new recovery form: itinerant rehab. Instead of a bricks-and-mortar institution, Acorn was administered out of Phil's apartment, and instead of complementary medical and counseling staffs, Acorn's staff was essentially Phil and Mary. (The third founder departed after Phil and Mary added a love angle to their partnership.)

Sessions continued to be offered wherever enough people wanted them, though as time went by, activity narrowed to a few hotbeds, including southern New Jersey and Greater Boston. When I called, I was told the next event would be in southern Indiana, where Acorn had forged an affiliation with the Kentuckiana Federation for Eating Disorders Recovery.

So on Saturday, Dec. 4, 1999, I embarked on yet another emergency flight. Stripped of the overhead incurred by physical plant and medical treatment, the fee was $1,500 for five days, roughly 28 percent of the South Oaks rate, adjusted for inflation.

An introductory program was offered on my first evening in town, but I skipped it for one last feed, at the Roadhouse BBQ franchise across the lot from the Extended Stay America where I would spend the night. The next day, I followed that up with a barely more controlled lunch at a sports bar where I watched football until halftime, when I had to report or risk missing my ride.

The gathering point was a spacious Victorian in a Louisville neighborhood that the federation had converted to office and meeting spaces. When the dozen of us — including two locals, a half dozen from Jersey or Philadelphia, a trio from Chicago, and a fellow Bostonian — had arrived, we piled our luggage and ourselves onto a school bus for the ride across the Ohio River and into the milds of Indiana. It was approaching darkness when we pulled into the crushed-stone driveway of a largish gray chalet situated at the edge of a pine stand on a lightly settled country lane.

Phil and Mary took separate quarters on the ground floor, where the three male clients shared a bedroom as well; a fourth guy would join us two days in. The women were given the run of the upstairs.

We were a disparate group in almost every way: In addition to geographical diversity, we ranged from 18 to 60, a couple of us were African-Americans, and one of the women was a twig of anorexia while one of the guys was a diabetic and well over 400 pounds; he'd be dead within a couple of years, having been unable to arrest his decline.

Our ranks included a hospice worker, a high school teacher, a speech pathologist, two therapists, an art-education student, and a wealthy suburban housewife whose husband and family had no idea that she purged up to 40 times a day.

It may or may not be coincidence that practically everyone was in a helping profession. But what we certainly had in common was that we were all control freaks who had lost enough control that we were willing to pay, in time and money, to try to get it back.

Whereas I had arrived at South Oaks determined to get what I came for, what I brought to Indiana was a seething anger. The part I could identify was directed at the copy desk staff, my boss, and her bosses, all of whom competed for title of most unfair person ever.

But I was also quite angry at myself. I distinctly remember, during the bus ride, chastising myself for having gotten into such a squeeze again. "I'm supposed to know this shit already!" I muttered in bitter self-reproach. The fear was paired with a desperation I hadn't had in advance of South Oaks, largely because now I had experienced recovery, however imperfectly, and I understood what I had to lose.

That didn't translate into my being very malleable, however. Before our first meal, Phil and Mary called us into the day room and laid out the ground rules, one of which was that we would all follow the same food plan. Immediately I balked. I had a perfectly good food plan, I grumbled, and it worked just fine when I followed it.

Within a couple of months, when I would meet my new nutritionist, Theresa Wright, I would learn that on the facts, I was completely wrong about that. But I was wrong in spirit, too. What good was it to go to all these lengths for help and then to argue with the helpers?

You might have thought I had finally learned that lesson at South Oaks, but that was going to be one of my themes for the week, learning that I knew a lot less than I thought I had learned.

Mary also laid out the house rules, which included that we not only would be preparing our own meals, but swishing our own toilet bowls and emptying our own trash. Staff had handled such things at South Oaks, but here, we would have to take responsibility for our upkeep.

The next morning, when she observed my breakfast routine, Mary asked me to measure the milk I used in my cereal, and asked how I'd feel about that.

"Resigned," I said.

"You seem angry to me," she said.

A little later, I wrote about that and added this: "I feel like I'm on the edge, and I can't imagine I'll make it through the week without exploding. The effort it will take to keep it in, under the prodding sure to come, and what's the point, anyway? I'm supposed to let it out. Why go, if I'm not going to let go? Regardless, I'm going to hold on as long as I can."

This is insanity by the numbers! 1) I need help. 2) I know where to get it. 3) I have only a narrow span in which to do it. 4) I'm going to hold out as long as possible, regardless.

After breakfast and chores, we embarked on what would be our daily routine, a mixture of education and therapy in a bright, sizable room with a large, cream-colored sectional, a few folding chairs, and an easel for Phil's lectures. First up, though, was community meeting, in which all the petty complaints and quotidian details of the day would be aired.

Sometimes the meeting would last five minutes, and sometimes it would dominate the morning, since at any time during an Acorn intensive, any comment, action, or feeling can lead to therapeutic activity.

If, for example, someone criticized how breakfast was prepared, the facts or style of the criticism might provide an opportunity to "do some work," whether for the cook or the critic. And that person's work might bring up strong reactions from others, who would then have their own work to do.

Whenever the meeting concluded, we would break and then reconvene for a lecture on addiction or for a "process group." In the latter, someone would take the floor to engage in psycho- or sociodrama to address some issue that they'd brought from home or that had arisen since arrival.

Based on something I'd said, Phil suggested early in the first process group that I "do" a tantrum, a specific assignment that is as it sounds, to stand in the middle of the circle and jump up and down, or writhe on the floor, or otherwise abandon adult control while railing against some injustice. For me, he suggested something to the effect of, "I don't wanna!"

But I didn't wanna.

I was the type to be vocal in the community meeting — because, after all, I knew better than everyone else — but for fear of embarrassment and less invested in getting well than in how I looked, I refused.

For that reason or just on my general comportment, I quickly became regarded as Angry Guy, and I began to feel estranged. This had been a theme since childhood: Enter a new community and soon alienate those I would have drawn close to. And once it went sour, it hardly ever got better.

After the first day's work but before dinner, I picked up where I'd left off in my journal, which can be a great companion when you're busy shunning those who don't want to talk to you:

"I'm confident now I can hold out. In the afternoon session, one of the peers shared her secrets" — another Acorn standard arising out of the dictum, "we're only as sick as our secrets" — "and one of them is that she's afraid of my anger and rage. Later, during feedback, three people (well, two, plus Mary) shared how they were glad she shared that.

"So three of them — out of nine others — are on the record as being afraid of me. Not exactly a safe place to let it out. I wasn't nuts about the crowd before, and now, well now there's nothing. Been here less than 24 hours and it already seems a wasted trip, a wasted leave, a waste of 2 grand."

And then I put down my pen, put on my jacket, and walked out.

Our bedroom had French doors to the outside, and I used them so I wouldn't have to explain to anyone what I was doing. In that moment, I really thought that I was going. Like, not coming back. Getting back to Louisville somehow, getting on a plane, and never looking back.

It wasn't much of a strategy: I left all my belongings, including my wallet. My coat was no match for the gray December weather. I had no idea where in rural Indiana I was or how I would get back to Louisville. But I stalked off in the direction I thought we'd come, nevertheless.

I bitched, brooded, and bemoaned, bringing to mind an incident from my teens when I'd bolted from Camp Kingsmont, the second summer fat farm I'd been sent to. I'd walked away from there, too, wanting what I wanted now, to be missed, to be wanted, to be rescued.

Forty-two years old, still adrift.

I made it perhaps three-quarters of a mile down the road on such thoughts, and then I began to realize the desperation of my situation. Matters of cold, no cash, and no clue of my whereabouts were important, but they couldn't compare to the real implications of my walkout:

➤— I wasn't screwing with insurance money anymore, and I couldn't afford to throw away the $1,800-plus I had invested.

➤— I'd been given sick time off to attend. How many times was the company going to approve that, especially when they found out I'd squandered the last one?

And even those two super-factors paled next to this:

 I needed the help!

I had been eating out of control for at least six months, and I hadn't been consistently healthy around food for years before that. I had few treatment options, and even fewer that I was willing to submit to. If I walked out on this one, who knew when I might find another place?

So I turned around, geographically if not yet spiritually. (Just because I had nowhere to go didn't mean I was willing to accept help.) I re-entered through the French doors but made no move to join the group, which had just sat down to dinner and was just realizing that I wasn't there.

First they called out. Then they sent a peer who tried to cajole me into joining them, but I said no. But your dinner, she said. I don't care, I said. I didn't say, but might as well have, that I was going to hold my breath until I turned blue.

Here I was, wanting to be rescued, telling my rescuer to go pound sand. And, I was going to punish her, all of them, by not eating my dinner! How's that for insanity in a compulsive eater? She had barely recrossed the threshold when I started regretting having blown my chance for dinner.

I was pretty surprised when, perhaps 10 minutes later, Phil came in with a tray of weighed and measured food. I didn't make it easy for him, but he did, after all, come bearing food, so eventually I let him give me what I so desperately wanted: permission, from myself, to rejoin the group.

He also left me with an assignment, to write about the people I was angry or sad about. I began with the peers who'd talked about my anger, but they were only the first in a wave of women, eight of them before I hit a guy, and that didn't even include the girlfriend who'd moved to Vermont just when things were getting good.

━◄▮►━

Phil Werdell might not be where he expected to be when he was a free-spirited radical of academia in the 60s, but few who hear his experiences are surprised he has spent decades helping problem eaters and evangelizing for food addiction. He has the heart of a helper and the constitution of a contrarian.

Though he has a history of problem eating himself, he's been like a rail as long as I've known him. His face is angular, sometimes grizzled, and it is topped by fine, thinning hair. His ever-present spectacles sit beneath an animated brow evidently vital to whatever point he's making.

And he makes a lot of them. He loves to talk.

On Tuesday morning, he presented his treatise on the "disease concept of food addiction," whose tenets include the ideas that it is chemically based, progressive, and chronic, so that even people who have arrested the symptoms for a period of time, as I had, are never cured.

He also presented what he called seven scientific theories about addiction, conceding that each of the seven was less scientific than its predecessor. The last was the one that has stuck with me: Addiction is nature's signal of a spiritual problem, in the way that pain from, say, a broken arm is nature's signal of a physical problem.

OK, so the science on this point is lacking. Non-existent, even. But my experience is that the spiritual steps I've taken to address my addiction have been central to my successes, and my belief is that it is not coincidental.

The other point Phil made that morning was profound in its utter practicality: "If, when you measure out your yogurt and you get a smear on your finger, wipe it off instead of licking it off."

Few statements about recovery have ever been more useful or meaningful, though I imagine many readers are rolling their eyes right about now, incredulous that this is wisdom. But it is, and here's how:

I did not go from the abstinence, serenity, and joy that followed South Oaks to the abusive late-night binges that preceded Acorn overnight, and I certainly didn't wake on any morning and decide that this would be the day I would return to bingeing. Most mornings I said specifically the opposite, that this wouldn't be the day.

I was mystified how I'd gotten so low again, and the answer, figuratively at least, was one smear of yogurt at a time. It wasn't a volume issue: If I had saved up every accidental smear from an entire year, it wouldn't have amounted even to a cup.

But the way I'd progressed around food was to have specific boundaries and the discipline to honor them. In this case, no matter how anal it sounds, the standard was one cup. Not one cup plus whatever got onto my finger.

If that smear was fair game, then so would the last bit of carrot that didn't fit into the measuring cup at lunch, or the last spoonful of potato in the serving dish at night.

And, if that smear was fair game, then I might just start, "unwittingly," to have more smears, or slightly larger ones, so that the number of calories might become a second factor, beyond poor boundaries. Remember, poor boundaries around food was precisely how I got to be 365 pounds.

Before leaving the matter of boundaries, it's worthwhile to look at its backside, not only in service to all the eye-rollers, but to illustrate why food addiction can be viewed as one of the most pernicious of all addictions.

Black-and-white thinking is the addict's mentality, which can be a bar to recovery when one is still active. But an addict who finds the willingness can then rely on the same trait to stay clean: "Just don't drink," they say in AA.

How's that going to work for an addicted eater? Food addicts have to take the tiger out of the cage three times a day. I've read that some drinkers have tried "controlled drinking," and it hasn't been very successful. Eaters don't just have to try it; they must practice it to survive.

Having a food plan is an attempt to address that, and having clear boundaries is a key to its working. But the comfort of all or nothing is just out of reach.

Say your plan calls for a cup of rice. You want to have good boundaries, so you fill the cup, and to be extra careful, you scrape the dull edge of a knife over the cup to ensure no excess. But one of the grains sticks to the knife and is left upright so that some of it is in the cup, and some is over the rim.

Jeez! Now it's half a grain of rice? That's super-crazy, no? But I maintain that this point is not evidence of it. I'm saying that food addicts, unlike alcoholics and many others, have both to try for perfection and to accept that perfection is unattainable, and that the only tool left is a wholesome discipline.

The problem is, if we had any clue about wholesome discipline, we wouldn't be addicts.

One of my first topics for journaling that Thursday morning was deadline pressure, which, after 20 years in journalism, I was certainly used to. It was the last full day, and I hadn't thrown a tantrum. I had participated, such as when I read aloud my writing on those I was angry with, but I hadn't emoted.

When we gathered, Phil said I was preparing to blame everyone else for having this retreat fail for me.

He outed me for my way of withdrawing, which he called "the most powerful force in the room" for the way my sulking affected those around me. (Sounds familiar, no?)

He outed me for implying that I wanted to be drawn out of my isolation, and then refusing the help offered.

And he said that I sought to outfence people, insisting on being right instead of insisting on being healthy.

So many years later, I'm mystified that he did this. He's not a blustery guy, and to the extent that the Acorn process is ever confrontational, it's much more gentle than this sounds. But I believe it happened, and not only because it's what I recorded in my journal; he was right on all counts.

Also, it worked. After lunch, in a session designed for something else, I asked if I could read my anger roster once more, with feeling. "Actually, it wasn't much of a reading; more of an explosion" at my boss, I recalled in the airport the next afternoon. At Phil's insistence — I wouldn't have done it otherwise, for fear of hurting him — my outburst included pummeling a thick pad he used to absorb such blows.

When I was done railing against the boss, he asked me what else my anger might apply to, and even at the pain of cliché, I served up my mother. At considerable volume, what came out was, "I'm good enough. Why can't you just support me? I've been around the world. I work for one of the best newspapers in the country. I'm good enough the way I am. Why can't you change?"

When I had spent myself physically, I stood alone in the circle, sobbing quietly with my eyes closed, hoping ostrichlike that no one would see me. I was still embarrassed, but what had changed was that my embarrassment, a.k.a. my pride, was no longer in charge.

When I started journaling, I developed the practice of beginning each entry with what I was feeling, because I'd been shown how disconnected from my feelings I was. For the five days of my Hoosier retreat, the progression of my emotions in these entries is barely to be believed.

On Monday, I wouldn't even honor the practice, but the tone was sarcastic, directed toward myself.

On Tuesday, I was "disgusted, annoyed," which I followed up by recording my first thought that morning, literally before I opened my eyes: "Nope, not today either."

On Wednesday I started with, "Feeling pretty chipper, except for the part of me that isn't glad about being chipper," as if a downside of feeling better was having to admit it.

On Thursday, the most I could muster was "not sure at the moment," but the writing that followed enumerated several fronts on which I felt progress.

On Friday, I didn't get to write until I was in the airport, but my reflection included this: "Jesus, how can such change come in five days? From a hopeless drunk to this." I'd just called someone I knew at home, someone who knew Acorn, and asked her to mentor me upon my return. It was the first time in months I'd been willing to ask for that help.

I have one other anecdote from that trip, which I'm sure I should just keep to myself but it's too illustrative (or I'm too self-revealing).

Friday morning, I pooped for the first time all week. It was very dark, very smelly, and prodigious enough to need a plunger. I'm quite sure it was the physiological side of my outburst of the day before.

Boy, did I feel better.

7

Profit in Surrender

AFTER ALL THE SPIRITUAL REFERENCES I've made so far, you might expect me to say that my first spiritual experience was ethereal and life-changing. But it had nothing to do with recovery or even God, so far as I could tell.

It simply let me go on a diet.

It was August 1988, and I was at another high point on the scale, another low point in life. Twice previously I'd ridden the Atkins diet to a 100-plus-pound weight loss, and wished I could do it again. But if my ample flesh was willing, my will was weak, and my few feeble attempts had failed within weeks each time.

Then I had my revelation.

I had just merged onto the Massachusetts Turnpike, returning to Connecticut from a shared birthday dinner for Mama Ruth and me; our birthdays are two days apart and we'd celebrated jointly for many of my 31 years. I don't recall having binged at the meal, or during the visit, and I don't recall being particularly focused on my weight that day. In fact, I wasn't thinking of anything in particular as I moved through the darkness at 70 mph.

Suddenly, I knew I could diet again. It wasn't a decision, and it hadn't come from thought. I just knew: If I would go to the market and get the right foods, it would be like I'd never left. In an instant, I felt the momentum that usually came with months of success.

A couple of days later, I went to see Sting perform at a local amusement park and was turned back at the turnstile because of the food I was carrying, food I knew wasn't on their menu of fried dough and corn dogs. If this had been another of my recent attempts, that would have been enough to say, "Oh well, I tried. I'll start again Monday." Instead, I just didn't eat until I got back to the car.

I'm sure this seems ridiculous to those who can't identify: "Big deal. So you went without food for a few hours." And on the first level, it's no bigger than that. But this was different because I knew, quite unreasonably, that I'd be taken care of.

Many people call that faith. But if you had said that to me then, I would have objected. Even while I was experiencing it, I would have insisted that faith was for losers, that God was a capricious bastard, and that religion was the illusory opiate of bovine, fearful, and weak people who needed a crutch to get through their sorry lives.

I actually said that one day while shooting the breeze around the copy desk, which quite offended a meek, church-going colleague. The anecdote sticks in my memory not only because he was upset, but because I was surprised he was upset. Hey, we were just talkin', y'know?

Insensitivity was only the beginning of my outrageous hubris: Like I had a better plan? Like I wasn't leaning on a hundred crutches myself and still unable to move? Could anyone have been less entitled to pontificate about the path to happiness? But hey, that's who I was, y'know?

It wasn't as though I hadn't had religious training. I am Jewish by birth and heritage, and if hours in temple or Hebrew school were the only requirements, I would be Jewish in ritual, too. I attended Hebrew School three times a week for eight years, and attended a Saturday morning service for students as well. One year, I was one of two pupils recognized for having missed neither a class nor a service.

Incredibly, though, I had never connected my religious training with God. When I was bar-mitvahed, I belted out the prayers, but to me they were tunes and syllables devoid of meaning. Even if I had understood the Hebrew, I expect I would still have missed the connection to God.

Not feeling any call, I haven't returned to a temple for worship since I left for college. As I proceeded through my 20s, I concluded that God didn't exist and that if he did, he was an ass. If he could make everything OK for everyone, why didn't he? (I have an answer that satisfies me now, but I get ahead of myself.)

At most, God was an intellectual topic, something to banter through the night while we passed a pot pipe. It certainly didn't matter, not to me. That is, it didn't matter until Ed Lafreniere called me into his office to suggest that I get help. That led to the employee assistance program, which led to talk of the "Higher Power" that I would have to confront in practically any rehab program I chose. To me, it was completely out of the question.

"Sure, I might need to make some changes," I sputtered to the counselor, "but if I start thinking God exists, that would be changing ... everything!" It would take a couple more years before I was ready even to countenance God talk, but it's clear to me now that I was absolutely correct that day: I would have to change everything if I was going to escape the pit I'd been wallowing in.

And I have.

Like so many other facets of my story, I didn't go easily. Instead of merrily skipping toward the Lord — do people do that? — I fought and clawed against what I was convinced was a phony construct of man: You can't see him — no one has ever seen him — but he's there. No, really.

At South Oaks, guidance toward spirituality emphasized the 12 Steps. (From what I understand, members can't identify themselves publicly, but I've never been a member of AA, so I feel free to talk about them.) I thought some of the steps had real merit, but before I could get to those, I'd have to deal with the ones about a "Higher Power."

At first I just tried thinking harder, which couldn't get me past what was squarely a spiritual question, but did produce some progress nevertheless, mostly after I'd left South Oaks as still a godless heathen.

Step 2 — "Came to believe in a Power greater than ourselves who could restore us to sanity" — seemed insurmountable to me at first; hell, just the first three words summoned sour tidings. But eventually I climbed through a loophole the width of a single letter, the "c" in "could."

If it had been a "w," I couldn't have gone for it, because I felt sure that no power would ever help me — I was sure it never had, anyway. But I'd already conceded that I wasn't the highest power in the world, and I didn't have to stretch much further to concede that one of these other powers might be able to restore me, if it wanted to.

I didn't spend much time on the last part, "restore us to sanity," and it's just as well, because I wasn't sure I'd ever been sane in the manner these folks were talking about. If I had been, it had come to me too early for me to recognize or recall it, and then it had departed.

Loophole or not, it was enough to move ahead to Step 3 — "Made a decision to turn our will and our lives over to the care of God as we understood him" — where, in effect, I would have to turn that "could" into "would." I still needed to believe, and it still made no sense to me. I just couldn't see how changing my beliefs would change anything material.

I envisioned the so-called leap of faith as a leap from a cliff. The day before, the leaper had believed – as most people would – that doing so would splatter him on the rocks below. But the day after, simply because he had changed his belief of what would happen, some unseen hand was going to save him from certain death? Yeah, right.

And what about motivation? He had changed his belief because someone had said there was something in it for him? Who could respect, say, a civil rights advocate who joined a restricted club because it had upgraded its golf course? It wasn't that I was resolutely principled; my ethics could hardly have been more situational. But I had my standards, or thought I did anyway, and honest consistency was one of them.

I took one major step toward overcoming my misgivings when I took a spiritual friend's suggestion to read "When Bad Things Happen to Good People," by Harold Kushner. It's a slender volume whose basic suggestion is that God doesn't cause tragedies, but that God helps those stricken by sorrow to withstand it and eventually to move on.

I also carried my inquiries to a couple men of the cloth: Somewhere in the newspaper, I'd seen that a minister from the church a block from our house in Marblehead was now in Connecticut, and though our only personal contact had been when he'd picked me up hitchhiking once or twice, I called him and asked to visit.

I also sought out Jon Luopa, my brother and sister-in-law's Unitarian minister, a gently inviting guy whose tack — and my reaction — really surprised me. He had no dog in the hunt, and wondered, if God was a stumbling block, shouldn't I try out Rational Recovery, which he said was analogous to the 12 Steps without the God part? My reaction was to defend "my" process, revealing more investment in it than I realized.

In conversations with others, however, I continued to challenge believers. My mentor, Michael, a patient man, let me talk, but he also made clear his view that I wasn't going to be able to skirt this one; logic and discussion might shorten the distance, but I was going to have to leap if I was ever to reach the opposing shore.

Not long after, Michael made a suggestion that helped as much as the one to read Kushner: If I didn't have a concept of God that worked for me, I should make up my own. Someone so averse to pretense should have kicked that one out cleanly, but all this focus had softened me up, and without too much effort, I conceived a Higher Power that combined my uncles Albert and Joe, one from each side of my family.

I chose them because neither had ever said a cross word to me, both had always had time for me, and I knew intuitively that both of them liked and loved me, whether they'd ever said it or not. They made me feel special. I was sure that in any circumstance, they would have wanted the best for me, would have helped me to get there if I had asked, and wouldn't have scolded me if I'd fallen short.

God should be so good.

Though I didn't see them at the time, there were a couple of other commonalities: Neither ever married, a path I thought I was on, and they both lived in the shadows of more accomplished brothers. (My dad's father, Joseph, ran leather businesses on the North Shore, and he had employed Albert, just as Solly had employed Joe.)

I began to picture one or both of them on my shoulder when I craved help or comfort that I wasn't finding in everyday life. If I conjured only one of them, it was usually Joe, who was more involved in my life at an earlier stage. He used to take me with him when he'd go to fix a broken window or install a shower enclosure, and he was there the day I learned to ride a bike.

This was just a construct, of course; I'd made it up. And yet, I stuck with it, so it must have been doing something for me.

Then came the day I was sure of it.

I'd been smoking cigars, one of the more severe detours my compulsion had taken since I'd put down the food. Practically overnight, I'd changed from the cigar-smoker who didn't finish a five-pack to one who went through 50 in a week. Yes, that's seven stinky stogies a day.

I was smoking before hitting the floor in the morning, and I'd often let one extinguish on the nightstand as I retired. I reordered my work day so that I could hang outside a couple of times a day. I allowed this obviously unhealthy behavior on the grounds that I wasn't inhaling, which a) was never completely true, b) didn't prevent nicotine dependence regardless, and c) skipped over the fact that it was addictive behavior, a major flaw in itself.

Just as had happened with food, I did come to see, eventually, that I was out of control and would have to stop, but had been unwilling or unable to. That's powerlessness: wanting to do something but being unwilling or unable to.

Then, one day I pulled into the CVS parking lot to get my next box, leaving a stub smoldering in the ashtray. I went in, got my stash, and stood in line. But it was long, and I was impatient, so I decided to look around until the line subsided. As I was browsing, an alchemy within me combined the knowledge that smoking was bad for me with the certainty that Uncle Joe wouldn't want it for me. Just like that, I put the box back and walked out a free man.

It was just like that night on the turnpike: I'd walked in with one intention, and left with another, certainly not because I'd willed it, but perhaps because I hadn't.

In my little world of rules, I would have been entitled to finish off the stogie in the ashtray, but I let it go, and, miraculously, that was the end of them. It's true that I've backslidden briefly over the years, so nothing's permanent, but I'll never forget how Uncle Joe helped me quit.

It was an impressive feat for a dead man, particularly one who smoked cigars every day that I knew him.

I don't see Joe and Albert on my shoulder that often anymore. I needed them at the time and I love them for helping me — when they were alive and afterward — but rarely do I think of God as being outside myself anymore.

I have come to believe that God tucked a piece of himself into me when I was dispatched to Earth, just as he did for each of us. I think we're all God-like at birth — I'm fond of Sinead O'Connor's lyric that "all babies are born saying God's name" — and that the goal is to stay that way while here.

But, probably for everyone and probably by design, that's a challenge. Life deals out its nicks and scrapes, and as the scar tissue thickens, it muffles the voice of God. I imagine my spiritual practices as a lotion that, when applied in a thousand dabs, dissolves those callouses and lets me get closer to God again.

I think that we all return to him eventually, but that growth is defined by how we deal with the challenges. Just as I borrowed from O'Connor above, I cadged this corner of my credo from that noted philosopher, Albert Brooks, expressed in his brilliant film "Defending Your Life." Its premise is that when we die, we go to a way station to be evaluated for how well we've overcome our fears. If we're found to have done well, we move on to another plane of existence, and if not, we're sent back to try again.

Though I am convinced that fear is a condition of lesser spiritual development, I fall just shy of literal acceptance of Brooks's premise. The truth is, of course, that I don't know what happens after death; I think not knowing is part of God's plan. I think that for his own reasons, God has decided not to reveal that and other parts of his design, that he has universal truths — gravity is constant, charity is good, thievery is wrong, etc. — but he wants us to learn them rather than just handing them to us. In fact, I would add that to the list of universal truths: Lessons learned are more valued than answers given.

It's still a source of amazement, or at least amusement, that what I once cited as evidence of God's cruelty — that he could make everything swell for everyone but refused to — is now a lesson that I should look for alternate explanations when something seems out of whack.

My transition to the internal God included adopting regular prayer, well before I believed in the exercise, at South Oaks. But in my typically stubborn way, I was still fighting it into the mid-'90s. A mentor I had for a while after moving to Boston, a dour man with a clear and steady voice of recovery, advised me to "Ask for help in the morning, and then say thanks for it at night." I did the first part but I held out on the back end. I don't know how long it took before I finally adopted his suggestion completely, but it was well after we'd parted ways.

What I pray for has also changed over time. I don't think I ever was in the please-God-can-I-have-a-million-dollars-and-Cameron-Diaz school, but I know I have tried to cloak my selfish schemes in acceptable language, as if I might fool the Almighty with my cleverness. Now I ask for help in my relationships with my loved ones, and ask for help to become more like the person I think God wants me to be: patient, tolerant, loving, and kind, among other attributes.

I also pray for others, in two general camps: The larger group is people who've suffered pain, and though what I really want is for God to make it all better, my request is that they be helped to move beyond it. The other group comprises those against whom I have resentments, which I took on as the result of a suggestion. It doesn't work on command, and sometimes doesn't work at all, but I have seen resentments melt away from this action.

I used to cop resentments toward God when the relief I sought didn't come, or didn't come fast enough. But now I have two answers for that; one is vastly more significant than the other.

The first one is that I am not in charge of the timing of God's grants, any more than I am in charge of the grants themselves. So the fact that I haven't received my answer may mean only that I haven't received it yet, perhaps because I haven't learned the lesson it heralds.

The second one not only undercuts the first, but could be interpreted as undercutting the entirety of prayer, and yet for me it doesn't, which is why I like it so: Even if God is listening to my prayers, he's not using my entreaties to determine his actions. If God has any steering role in my life — itself a doubtful proposition — he certainly knows what I need before I do.

So why bother praying then, if no one is on the other end of the line? Great question. At points like this, in earlier days, that I would reject the whole scheme as a scam. The measure of the changes within me is that even if it is nonsensical to me, I do it anyway.

I have seen that prayer works in my life, regardless of how it works. The image I have is of me, extending my hand through a curtain and depositing whatever request I have on the other side. It seems not to matter whether that request is sent for further processing or if it lies there forever. The key act is my letting it go.

Maybe it's self-hypnosis: I ask for help, say, to be more tolerant, and over time, tolerance moves closer to my core, more easily deployed the next time I'm about to react to the idiot next to me. Could be. But the point is, I no longer require understanding a process to get benefit from it.

The logic of praying for matters outside of me is even dicier: How can my friend Chris, for example, whose mom just died, get any benefit from my praying that he be given solace and support? Well, first, I do see the same benefit as in my example of tolerance above: If I'm praying for him, he's more likely to come to mind when I'm thinking of reaching out to someone in need.

But I also consider the notion of collective consciousness, and am willing to believe I can put vibrations into the world that have an effect elsewhere. I don't think it's true, I don't believe it's true, and I certainly have no evidence it's true. But I'm willing to accept the possibility.

Maybe praying for others belongs in the same category as funerals. When I go to one, one effect is that I get solace; when I pray for someone else, one effect is that I get help. What I've decided is that, regardless of what actually transpires, there's very little downside to any of the apparent or imagined outcomes, so why not?

Both believers and skeptics could fairly ask, "Where in all this thought is the faith?" which my tattered Webster's defines as "firm belief in something for which there is no proof"? I do the justice to "firm belief," but not to the rest: Even if what passes for proof in my life has hugely expanded as the result of my spiritual inquiries, I concede that my "faith" derives chiefly from observation, discussion, and reasoning. Even after all these years of "change," I'm still figuring, still trying to explain what's happening. Maybe I'll always be that way.

But perhaps I can claim faith anyway: Even today, I can easily argue why prayer can't work – I'm just whispering to myself at the edge of my bed, right? And yet, I do it anyway, not because I'm a slavish idiot but because I can see the benefits, even while I can't explain them.

My discussion so far has covered only my speaking with God. But communication, of course, is two-way. How do I know what God's will is if He's not engaged in my prayer?

I believe that God speaks to me through other people, which isn't too much of a leap for someone who believes that a piece of God is within each of us.

That doesn't mean that I hear every word from every person as the word of God; that's as absurd as when I piloted by childish moods and whims as if they were appropriate guides for living. Even after I started trying to follow God's will, the result sometimes was still chaos.

Now, I listen for consensus from others who are pursuing spiritual growth, especially if they came to it, as I did, through the door of food insanity. Yes, we could just all be crazy — nuttiness around food and body image is our common bond, after all. But when I gather regularly with others, I get to see the progress that people around me are making — or not making — which makes it easier to know whom to emulate. The common phraseology among my pals is, "Look for someone who has what you want and ask how he or she is achieving it."

The drawback to this method of discerning God's direction is that while it works wonderfully on a cumulative basis, I can't count on going to a particular group and leaving with particular guidance on a particular question. Nor can I count on a specific individual to give me the specific suggestion I need — not without making that person my Higher Power.

Somehow along my path, I devised a second way of divining God's will for me, which I'm sure isn't original. When I'm not certain what God would have me do, I reframe the question to, "what would love do?" Intellectually, equating God and love seems fair, and it has never led me astray or failed to translate.

I recognize its value when I think back to all the instances in which I wish I had been nicer. I can't think of any in which I wish I had been nastier. What would love do?

I am married to a wonderful woman, Georgina. Savvy, clever, valued in her profession, loving and loved deeply by so many. Any guy would be lucky to share his life with hers, but I almost wasn't the guy. Early in our acquaintanceship, she asked me point-blank if I wanted children.

"I know it's only our third date, but I don't want to find out two years from now, having invested all that time, that you don't, and that I have to start over," she said. God bless her for knowing herself, and for being able to state her truth, right?

I, on the other hand, had somewhat less clarity. My answer, had I been asked by a buddy or in a phone survey, would have been "no." I felt that I'd missed out on so much, having sacrificed so many years to my addiction, that now I just wanted to travel, to indulge, to play. But we were embracing, on a cobblestoned Boston street that gleamed from just-ended rain, and I allowed that, OK, I would consider it. I may have answered even a bit more affirmatively than that, though I wouldn't want to call it lying or anything so harsh.

Of course, the topic eventually rose again, on a ride home from a family visit to Vermont, and when I expressed my eagerness as somewhat south of what I'd said that night, I provoked a crisis in our relationship. As soon as I dropped Georgie off, I called my brother — my most trusted sounding board and advisor — and said I needed to see him. Immediately.

First thing next morning, I drove down to Connecticut and Rich escorted me onto his deck, sat me down, and listened. When I was done, he said he understood. "I heard your reasons, and I think you're clear about them. You don't want to be a parent, and she does. I think you should break up." Perhaps he was a bit more expansive, but that's what I remember.

His pronouncement had particular resonance because I still felt a slight sting from another time when I'd said I didn't want to be a parent, and he'd replied, "Oh, yeah? What are you doing that's so damned important?" But even without that, I was increasingly likely to heed Rich as the stakes of the question went up.

But not this time. On the way home, I started thinking about that "other" authority. God. What would God have me do?

What would love do?

And what I concluded was that I loved this woman. I'd seen all the ways we fit, all the ways in which she helped me, and let me help her. It seemed pretty clear that love had led me there. That meant, at least figuratively, that God had led me there. If my love for her meant I was going to be a father, perhaps that was what love would have me do.

I decided that even if I didn't like the outcome later, I would always know that I'd followed an honest and spiritual path, and that that was about as good as it was going to get, that no one gets guarantees.

As I write this, my 14-week-old son is asleep upstairs. Not only am I a parent, but I'm the primary caregiver, having left 28 years of pursuing daily journalism to raise this boy, in conjunction with Georgina. So far, the boy is pretty great, and I can see that it might turn out to be one of the most "damned important" endeavors of my life.

Never would I have mapped this path. Just the marriage part seemed unlikely for most of my life. But being a dad? Leaving my day job, when for most of my life it was my chief source of esteem? It all seems impossible. And pretty good.

I reached this point not because I designed it, but because I didn't. Because I let go of the reins, haltingly and irascibly, and only then because they said I'd lose weight. If they'd said it would lead me to this place, I wouldn't haven't believed it, even if I'd wanted it. But I have the faith — or is it the experience? — to keep asking what God would have me do, and to see what happens next.

Finally, a postscript to my meanderings, to make clear that I do not follow God's will or my own interpretations of it perfectly. Not only do I not think I'm a saint, neither does anyone else who has ever dealt with me regularly. I don't do any of this goody-goody-glorioski stuff perfectly, or even consistently. But what is supportable is that I act more in the image of God than I used to, a trend that is probably as close to spiritual perfection as I will ever get.

Sometimes my less God-like tendencies — sarcasm, harsh judgment, bitterness, gossip — are short-lived, but instances have persisted for years. Sometimes I've actually seen these defects as defects, and still been unable to change. (There, again, is powerlessness.) But when I become able to acknowledge the harm I'm doing — and the spiritual harm I'm bringing on myself — I have somewhere to go for help, to God and prayer.

8

Seven for Seven

THE FIRST DICTIONARY DEFINITION of the word "miracle" makes reference to divine intervention, and as it regards my experience, I wouldn't argue. There are two little miracles just in that sentiment, that I'll allow that a divinity exists, and that I'm not going to argue about it.

But the miracle I'm referring to is me.

Now, just to be painfully clear: I did not create this miracle. I have three decades of evidence to prove that when I was in charge of my life, I created more mayhem than miracle.

But I know there are those who will look at the details of my journey and, even if they are impressed, will scoff at God's supposed involvement. For them, I would point to the second definitions, such as this one from the Oxford American: "a highly improbable or extraordinary event, development, or accomplishment that brings very welcome consequences."

Still me.

To have gone from where I was to where I am is an entirely improbable, extraordinary development that has had very welcome consequences. But the key point of my story, and the key reason to share it with you, is that it's not **only** about me.

Yes, I had a timely intervention by co-workers, guidance to therapy, a shove toward problem-eater support groups and then toward rehab, a really big shove toward spirituality, and an endless reservoir of help and support from people who could relate with my struggles.

But all that could have happened to anyone. I know tons of people for whom such relief, and flowering, has come. Not everyone had an intervention or got to go to rehab for free, but they each found a portal to recovery, walked inside, and decided to stay.

My question is, in a nation where 2 of 3 adults have a weight problem: Why aren't more people finding relief?

Most folks you ask for weight-loss suggestions would answer with Weight Watchers or Jenny Craig, drugs or dietary supplements, gastric banding or gastric bypass. But what we know about all these "solutions," taken together, is that the problem they seek to address is worsening.

Clearly, we need a more effective approach. But just as clearly, I can't expect folks to buy my contentions about food addiction and treatment just 'cause I say so: The arguments should measure up to the scientific view of addiction **too**. If you've read this far, you already have all the facts to know that they measure up quite well, even if you don't realize it yet.

What lay people like us call an addiction is, in the parlance of the American Psychiatric Association, a substance use disorder, a term that covers both dependence and abuse of drugs, alcohol, amphetamines, caffeine, marijuana, nicotine, inhalants, opioids, sedatives, hallucinogens, and other substances.

Food is not recognized in that context, though two behaviors — anorexia and bulimia — are, and a third — binge-eating disorder — is a good bet to make it into the next edition, due out in 2013. But for the substances that are, the APA's Diagnostic and Statistical Manual of Mental Illness gives practitioners seven standards to assess whether a patient has a substance use disorder. Let's look at them one at a time, beginning with TOLERANCE, as in, Did I use more of the substance(s) over time to achieve the same result?

That's easy, right? I didn't start out eating two foot-longs on my visits to Subway, but I progressed to that. And the first "official" binge that I had after South Oaks, which I described in Chapter 5, was easily more food than a couple of foot-long sandwiches, with chips or without. Countless times, I would stop only when I couldn't accommodate another bite.

WITHDRAWAL is an easy concept to grasp: Does stopping the behavior produce physical symptoms? Most people, I think, would recognize the obvious irritability a smoker displays upon quitting, or the DTs (delirium tremens) that alcohol abusers experience when they stop drinking cold turkey. Food withdrawal is more subtle, but it is completely observable if you're looking for it.

I told one of my best examples in an anecdote in Chapter 6, when I told of binging practically to the moment I reported for my first Acorn workshop in 1999. My mood was so dark the first couple of days that I had decided to sit out the process I'd flown a thousand miles and spent almost two thousand dollars to engage in. But as the effects of sugary, high-fat, and high-volume food started to leave my system, I started to get better. On day 3, I told my journal that I was "feeling pretty chipper," and I did emotional work the next day.

Until I learned about the physical aspects of withdrawal, I'd always thought I was just being a baby and a jerk for acting as I did. OK, I **was** acting like a baby and a jerk, but it was based in physiology, not personality. So, by the way, was my little poop story from day 5 that closes out that chapter. My friend, the nationally recognized nutritionist Theresa Wright, tells me that the lining of the intestine sheds its cells every 3-5 days, and it wasn't until I got a new set accustomed to cleaner food (less processed, less sugar- and fat-laden) that I was able to do my business.

The next standard is UNINTENDED USE. It refers both to eating more food, and for a longer period, than planned at the start.

Anyone who's ever dieted can relate. One example is "slivering a cake to death," pledging to take one small slice, but then taking another, and then another. An example of my own is eating, with tacit permission, from friends' pantries while they were out, but going back to the bag or the box so many times that I had no choice but to go out and replace it to cover my tracks. That decision brought shame, but it also brought relief because I could just kill the whole thing instead of fretting over whether I could get away with "just one more," again. It also meant that on the way back from the store, I would get to eat down to where my host had left the package.

UNSUCCESSFUL EFFORTS TO CUT DOWN OR CONTROL USE is another softball: Every dieter I have ever met has decided, more than a few times, to start a new diet on Monday, or to cut back a little, or just to do a little better. But if those decisions had any force in the world, we wouldn't be having this discussion. When you consider that I've lost more than 130 pounds four times, it's clear that I made fairly heroic efforts to cut down or control. But not only did permanent weight loss not result, I usually started gaining the moment I stopped losing.

INORDINATE TIME AND EFFORT EXPENDED TO OBTAIN, USE, AND RECOVER FROM THE SUBSTANCE. This was my game plan on those nights I worked for the Telegraph in northeastern Ohio and even more vociferously by the time I'd reached the Courant in Hartford (both from Chapter 3): thinking about what I would get from the cafeteria or the vending machines to hold me until I could get to a mini-market after work; ensuring that I had purchased enough to get me through the night; eating through the wee hours; and waking up befogged but often still full.

IMPORTANT RECREATIONAL, SOCIAL, AND OCCUPATIONAL ACTIVITIES ARE SACRIFICED. I gave up many opportunities, in these three categories as well as others. I didn't recount it in detail in Chapter 5, but could there be a clearer example of forgoing a recreational activity than having planned a trip to the Jazz Festival in New Orleans, only to binge the night before and miss the plane?

Not only did I sacrifice hundreds of dollars for the apartment I'd rented and the flights I'd missed, but I robbed myself of experience as well — fabulous music, great food, and wild times. Still, I "chose" to stay up most of the night, bingeing. I use quotation marks because I didn't really "choose."

This is what powerlessness, in the addiction sense, looks like. If I was really choosing, I'd have acted differently.

A less grand example of the social type is when, as often as I could after I moved to Connecticut, I avoided the heartfelt entreaties of my brother and his wife to come for dinner. When I finally acceded, I'd leave early-ish, even if we were having a good time. The reason? The only McDonald's on the way home closed at 9, and more than the family connection, I valued the drive-thru.

For occupation, a story I didn't tell but could have, is when I flew to Florida, at the expense of the Fort Lauderdale Sun-Sentinel, for a weekend job interview. I was told to bring clips of my design work and appear at 9 a.m. on Saturday. But when I got in Friday night, I headed for the Publix market and binged big time, killing a half-gallon of ice cream, a box of cereal with milk, and who knows what else. I overslept, of course, really rankling the editor who'd come in early on his day off expressly to meet me. He was even less impressed when I told him I'd left the clips at home.

Later, he told me that if his choice had been based strictly on the copy-editing test, or the clips, I "would have been the guy." But my actions had made clear I wasn't.

CONTINUED USE DESPITE KNOWING THE ILL EFFECTS WOULD WORSEN. Again, too obvious! This is what compulsive eaters do — we know we're hurting ourselves, but can't/don't stop anyway.

At South Oaks, I barely overlapped with a guy who was deemed suicidal because he had developed diabetes and was still eating sugar. Nor have I forgotten Jimbo and Jerome, two fun, colorful compulsive eaters I shared time and experiences with in support groups. Neither was able to stop despite knowing they were courting early death, and they died within a year of each other.

That, ladies and gentlemen, is seven for seven. The APA has seven standards for assessing a substance use disorder, and all seven apply to me. The obvious question is: If it's so obvious by the APA's own guidelines, why is it that most doctors, as well as the public at large, have no clue?

There are plenty of good answers, including how doctors are trained: The focus is on fixing the sick, rather than promoting wellness. (Dr. Andrew Weil once opined that to the academic mind, "nutrition looks like home economics.")

But a point more specific to addiction and food is that the term "food" is very encompassing compared, say, to alcohol; I don't know of any alcoholics who can't drink beer but can drink wine, or whatever. It's a yes-or-no question. Same with cocaine: Whether it's powder, rock, or main-lined, coke addicts can't do coke, period.

Food addicts must eat, of course, so already, we're in a different category. But that's just the beginning of the differences.

When some people hear "food addiction," they think, "Oh sure. What's next, air addiction?" And though I know they don't understand, I understand the reaction. But what are we going to call it: "some-food addiction"?

Clearly, we're not, but even then, it wouldn't cover all the permutations. The first time I over-ate after South Oaks, it was a few fistfuls of lettuce. I don't say that lettuce is addictive. Nor do I say even that lettuce is addictive for me. The point is that my addiction includes behaviors, not just substances: I had a food plan, and that lettuce was outside my boundaries, so for me, it was addictive eating.

Adding to the confusion is that no food I'm aware of is addictive for all food addicts; that's the departure from alcohol, coke, et. al. As I've said, many have trouble with refined sugar and refined starches (aka flour), but I know plenty of self-identified food addicts who eat one or both. I avoid those substances, not to be puritanical but because I feel better when I do. I've also identified a raft of other foods that have led to me to fits of binge-ing often enough to rule them out. For me, these substances are addictive. And I can eat substances that others can't.

Then, of course, is the fact that not all obese people are food addicts. Some merely developed poor eating habits. Others, meanwhile, are eating over emotional trauma. If those people get the proper nutritional and/or emotional counseling, they can become normal eaters again.

But if they keep on, many will cross into addiction, a biochemical sensitivity from which there is no return. Maybe they were born with a tendency toward addiction — Dr. Ernest Noble and his UCLA team identified a genetic addiction link in 1994, and an avalanche of research has followed — or maybe they weren't. I know plenty of people who have concluded they were addicts from the womb.

The question of how we got there is less important than what we're going to do about it. Clearly, if the problem is chronic, a "diet," as defined by the mainstream, isn't going to resolve it. The guidance I've received and the experiences that have resulted tell me that I not only need to change how I eat, but how I approach many facets of life.

One's prescription can seem extensive — even overwhelming, depending on an individual's circumstance — and I can imagine the prospects exciting few people of any stripe. Lots of eaters are going to balk at abstaining, but to learn that recovery is going to require rigorous honesty, or more attention to spirit, could be far more off-putting.

Then again, who gets excited about any serious treatment prescription? Certainly not the cancer patient told she'll have to undergo radiation, or the back patient ordered to a month's uninterrupted bed rest, or the lung patient told he'll need a double transplant.

To some, the flaw of those comparisons will be their being equated with food addiction, and that is the rub, entirely. The medical profession and the public at large don't see that they are equivalent. The consequences of obesity (the chief consequence of food addiction) constitute the fastest-growing, and soon the gravest, threat to public health. Obesity is suicide on lay-away: It has plenty of time to degrade quality of life before finally ending life prematurely. Is that not pretty serious?

Meanwhile, let's consider alternative explanations why so many people are fat. Remember: More than one third of American adults, in the neighborhood of 70 million, are considered obese (having a body mass index greater than 30), and a slightly smaller group is considered overweight (having BMIs between 25 and 30). (Among children, the rate of overweight is 1 in 3.)

Are we really going to explain those circumstances entirely on personal choice? People can do whatever they want, and they are choosing to suffer the pain, isolation, embarrassment, and curtailment of normal living that obesity brings? All 145 million of them? It just beggars belief.

Without doubt, poor personal choices — some even arising from indolence and sloth, if that makes you feel better — contribute greatly to the obesity numbers, and just as I have been responsible for my choices, so is everyone else. But it is biological fact that substance misuse and addiction are different, and the difference is choice: I chose to misuse, but once I crossed into addiction, I abused food — abused myself with food — no matter what my intentions were.

For a moment, let's say that I'm wrong about food addiction, that the ubiquity or necessity or chemistry of food makes it essentially different from "real" addictions. Even if that's true, I still got all the goodness that resulted from my treating myself as an addict, broad and deep riches that I hadn't even tasted in three decades of thrashing about.

Swayed by my experience, I have sometimes argued that it doesn't even matter if food addiction exists. The existential truth of it isn't what got me well; it was the treatment.

The problem is that until medical and popular perception changes to reflect the peril that millions of Americans are facing, most people won't even know they should explore the questions, never mind be willing to take substantial steps to put their lives on different paths.

When I got willing, I went from isolated and barely dateable to husband and father, from inconsistent man-child to trusted colleague and friend, from creaky couch creature to cyclist and jogger (though not a very fast one). I have experienced growth, happiness, and serenity in ways I hadn't fathomed.

Wisely guided or merely hoodwinked, I accepted the methods of addiction treatment and I got better. Since, as I've observed before, I'm just not that special, if it happened for me, it can happen for millions of others who struggle with food the way I struggled.

And aren't results the crux of the discussion? We talk about solutions for obesity, and yet the methods most widely used are not reducing the problem! Isn't that how "solutions" earn their name, by solving?

I don't say that I approved of the steps before embarking. I don't say they were easy, or palatable. I don't say I did them enthusiastically. What I say is that I have a 150-pounds-plus weight loss that is approaching two decades. What I say is that within the flexible bounds of human experience, I'm happy, hopeful, active, and eager for whatever comes next.

Who doesn't want some of that?

APPENDIX A

Food Plan

I would prefer not to detail what I eat, because it doesn't really matter. Having a plan of eating and following it — respectfully and rigorously — is far more important than what the plan says.

Of course, there are limits. If I rigorously and respectfully follow a food plan that calls for 2 ounces of whipped cream at breakfast, a bushel of apples at lunch, and anything for dinner as long as it's round, I'm not going to achieve the healthy balance I need.

This is also true if I eat only "healthy" foods, but in unbridled quantities and whenever I want; you could call that a food plan too. But having a plan so that I'm not eating on whim has brought me important value separate from nutrition.

The following plan was prescribed for me by H. Theresa Wright of Renaissance Nutrition in East Norriton, Pa., one of the leading nutritionists in the country. She understands food addicts better than any non-food addict I've ever met.

Theresa has been prescribing my food plan since 2000, when I came to her, somewhat under duress imposed by a mentor, Susan, who insisted a) that I have a nutritional guide, and b) that it not be Susan herself. This was in the week or two after I'd left the Acorn workshop in southern Indiana. I'd insisted on following my own food plan while there, maintaining that it worked when I followed it. I was convinced that the fault lay not in the plan but in myself.

Then I met Theresa.

She began by asking about the plan I'd been following (or trying to follow), since I'd received it at South Oaks eight years prior. After assessing it to be about 1,600 calories a day, she told me that I had, in effect, been starving myself. She followed that lightning bolt by telling that she was going to prescribe a plan that was about 2,200 calories — more than a third more — and I would not only stabilize my eating but lose weight. It seemed like voodoo to me, at once both tantalizing (more food!) and foreboding (more food?). But that's just what happened.

Unlike the two-sizes-fit-all plan I got at South Oaks (one for men, a smaller one for women), my plan has changed numerous times over the years. Under the first plan, I ate four times a day; I'm now up to six. Lunch and dinner used to include a cup of starch; it later fell to three-quarters of a cup, and now I am down to half a cup. Every change resulted from my bringing a concern to Theresa and her devising an alternative I could live with.

The point is that this is only a snapshot of a plan that keeps changing, designed for me and not for you. I don't say that because I'm unwilling to share; it's because what's right for me isn't necessarily right for you.

Nevertheless, I know that some readers will want to know, specifically, what I'm eating, both in proportion and in detail. So with all my provisos, here it is:

Breakfast	1 cup yogurt or milk fruit (6 oz., 1 cup, or medium size) 1 cup grain (cooked) or 1 oz. grain (dry)
Morning snack	2 oz. protein fruit (6 oz., 1 cup, or medium size)
Lunch	4 oz. protein 1/2 cup starch 3 cups raw vegetables or 2 cups cooked. or 1 cup each of raw and cooked 2 tsp. fat (about 10 grams)
Afternoon snack	2 oz. protein fruit (6 oz., 1 cup, or medium size)
Dinner	Same as lunch
Evening snack	1 oz. grain fruit (6 oz., 1 cup, or medium size)

Here's how a typical day looks, with details filled in:

Breakfast	1 cup of yogurt (plain, low fat, sugar-free) 1 cup banana (fresh) and cherries (frozen), whipped into the yogurt 1 cup oatmeal
Morning snack	Apple 2 oz. cheese
Lunch	4 oz. grilled chicken 1/2 cup curried brown rice 1 cup carrots in tomato sauce, cooked 1 cup roasted peppers 2 tsp. butter
Afternoon snack	2 oz. cheese 1 pear
Dinner	4 oz. grilled shrimp 1/2 cup black beans 1 cup ratatouille 1 cup sautéed asparagus 2 tsp. butter
Evening snack	3 rice cakes 6 oz. grapes

APPENDIX B

Support

TREATMENT | **Acorn Food Dependency Recovery Services**
Box 50126
Sarasota, FL 34232-0301
941-378-2122
foodaddiction.com

Milestones In Recovery
2525 Embassy Drive South, Suite 10
Cooper City, FL 33026
800-347-2364
milestonesprogram.org

Shades of Hope
Box 639
Buffalo Gap, TX 79508
800-588-4673
shadesofhope.com

TREATMENT CONTINUED	**Turning Point of Tampa** 6227 Sheldon Road Tampa, FL 33615-3100 813-882-3003 tpoftampa.com
NUTRITION	**Lori S. Herold, RD** Dietitian, Turning Point of Tampa 3629 Justin Drive, Palm Harbor, FL 34685 727-791-7200 Ext. 5 tpoftampa.com **Lisa Merrill MS, RD, CDE** 21641 Allen Road, Woodhaven, MI 48183 1112 Catalpa, Royal Oak, MI 48067 734-502-8264 lisa@lisamerrill.com lisamerrill.com **H. Theresa Wright MD RD LDN** Renaissance Nutrition Center 2500 DeKalb Pike; Suite 200 East Norriton, PA 19401 610-275-3699 sanefood.com
COUNSELING	**Linda W. Boynton** 264 Beacon St., No. 401 Boston, MA 02116 617-262-2112 **Kris White** Mystical Therapies 378 S. Main St. Haverhill, MA 01835 978-372-5300 mysticaltherapies.com

SUPPORT GROUPS

Anorexics and Bulimics Anonymous ABA
Main P.O. Box 125
Edmonton, Alberta, Canada T5J 2G9
anorexicsandbulimicsanonymousaba.com

Compulsive Eaters Anonymous CEA-HOW
5500 East Atherton St., Suite 227-B
Long Beach, CA 90815-4017
562-342-9344
ceahow.org

Eating Disorders Anonymous (EDA)
General Service Board of EDA, Inc.
Box 55876
Phoenix, AZ 85078-5876
eatingdisordersanonymous.org

Food Addicts Anonymous (FAA)
World Service Office
4623 Forest Hill Blvd. Suite109-4
West Palm Beach, FL 33415-9120
561-967-3871
foodaddictsanonymous.org

Food Addicts In Recovery (FAIR)
foodaddictsinrecovery.com
Note: No central phone or address; based in Houston

Food Addicts in Recovery Anonymous (FA)
400 West Cummings Park, Suite 1700
Woburn, MA 01801
781-932-6300
foodaddicts.org

Greysheeters Anonymous
GSAWS, Inc.,
Prince Street Station
Box 630 New York, NY 10012
greysheet.org

SUPPORT GROUPS
CONTINUED

Obsessive Eaters Anonymous (OEA)
Box 7555
Glenageary, Co. Dublin Ireland
353-[0]1-289-1599
obsessiveeatersanonymous.org

Overcomers Outreach (OO)
12828 Acheson Dr.
Whittier, CA 90601
800-310-3001
overcomersoutreach.org
Note: Deals with problem eating, but other issues as well

Overeaters Anonymous (OA)
World Service Office
Box 44020
Rio Rancho, NM 87174-4020
505-891-2664
overeatersanonymous.org

Recovery from Food Addiction (RFA)
Box 35543
Houston, TX 77235
713-673-2848
RFAworldservice@aol.com

ADVOCATES

Binge Eating Disorder Association
550M Ritchie Hwy. #271
Severna Park, MD 21146
443-597-0066
bedaonline.com

Food Addiction Institute
Box 50126
Sarasota, FL 34232-0301
fai@foodaddiction.com

Food Addiction Professionals
5535 Memorial Drive F814
Houston, TX 77007
713-446-3663
refinedfoodaddiction.org